Confront Your Comfort, Excel in Your Press:
Reaching Your Why, Your Vision & Your Victorious Place

2nd Edition

Shannon T. White, MSW, LCSW, Mindset Coach

Copyright © 2019, 2020 Shannon T. White
All rights reserved. This book is protected under the copyright laws of the United States of America. It may not be copied or reprinted without written permission of the author, granted upon request.

Info.ReigniteYourLife@gmail.com
ShannonTWhite.com

Cover Design: Spked Studios
www.SpkedStudios.com
Cover Photos: D. Michae' Photography
www.dmichae.com

1st Edition proofread by Joslyn Ryder and Tanya Campbell

2nd Edition proofread and updated by Ready Writer Services, LLC
www.readywriterservicesllc.com

Unless otherwise noted, all Scripture quotations marked (KJV) are taken from the King James Version public domain.

Scripture quotations marked (AMP) are taken from the Amplified Bible, Copyright © 2015 by The Lockman Foundation. Used by permission.

Scripture quotations marked (NIV) are taken from the Holy Bible, New International Version®, NIV®. Copyright © 1973, 1978, 1984, 2011 by Biblica, Inc.™ Used by permission of Zondervan. All rights reserved worldwide. www.zondervan.com The "NIV" and "New International Version" are trademarks registered in the United States Patent and Trademark Office by Biblica, Inc.™

Scripture quotations are from the ESV® Bible (The Holy Bible, English Standard Version®), copyright © 2001 by Crossway, a publishing ministry of Good News Publishers. Used by permission. All rights reserved.

Scripture quotations marked MSG are taken from THE MESSAGE, copyright © 1993, 2002, 2018 by Eugene H. Peterson. Used by permission of NavPress. All rights reserved. Represented by Tyndale House Publishers, a Division of Tyndale House Ministries.

ISBN: 978-0-578-67312-7
Independently published

DEDICATION

This book is dedicated to my grandmothers, Roberta Rivers and Viola C. Pendleton, whose examples of faith, love and strength helped to shape me into the resilient woman that I am today…whose prayers carried me into the discovery of my own gifts, talents and purpose. I am honored to carry the torch of their legacy & forever grateful that they accepted God's call on their lives as it concerned me.

Loving and thanking them, always and forever.

CONTENTS

	Acknowledgments	i
	Foreword	ii
	Introduction	iv
1	The Challenge	1
2	The WHY Factor	Pg 8
3	Identifying Your WHY	Pg 16
4	My Testimony.... The Road to My WHY	Pg 29
5	Outlining Your Daily Actions	Pg 44
6	The Choice	Pg 60
7	The Power of Your Mind	Pg 78
8	Building Mental Muscle	Pg 85
9	Visualize Your WHY	Pg 94
10	Equipped for the Press	Pg 104
	Afterword	Pg 114
	Appendix A: Mental Muscle Workout Plan	Pg 119
	Appendix B: Declarations and Scriptural References	Pg 125
	My Personal Declaration	Pg 129
	My Favorite Scriptures	Pg 131
	Additional Note Pages	Pg 133

ACKNOWLEDGMENTS

I would like to acknowledge some very special people who have been instrumental in the completion of this book.

My heartfelt thanks to my spiritual father and mother, Bishop John and Pastor Isha Edmondson. Your obedience to the call on your life directly influenced my desire to press towards my own. God truly used your ministry to show me what it means to be the righteousness of God. Without that knowledge, this book would not exist.

Special thanks to my rope-holders (you know who you are). Your love and encouragement pushed me out of my comfort zone, inspired me in the press and LITERALLY helped me birth this spiritual baby when the labor pains got intense. I could not have made it through any of the sleepless nights, nor emotional days, without your consistent prayers, empowering conversations and selfless sacrifices. I am eternally grateful.

And most of all, thank you to my five reasons for wanting nothing more than to complete this God-given assignment… my amazing husband, Glen, and my beautiful children, Aniiya, Amin, Elyon and Shawn. You are truly God's tangible expression of His love for me. You make me BETTER… pushing me past my limits and into my Victory!

Shannon T. White, MSW, LCSW, Mindset Coach

FOREWORD

In a world of high stress, setbacks and personal demands; many people (if totally honest with themselves) will admit that their behaviors and self-talk do not reflect the vision of success that they dream of having, nor the calling on their lives that innately defines who they were created to be. As a result, they find themselves "comfortable"; subject to mediocre thinking and hesitant or fearful of taking action.

They often make excuses to justify their stagnation and become accustomed to operating with a very limited perspective of their capabilities. As a result, goals, projects and assignments are often left unfinished; relationships are underdeveloped; potential gets aborted and they find themselves settled in their comfort zone and/or plain "stuck". Despite many attempts to identify and live out their purpose or finish what they start, they lack direction and/or the wisdom to get back on track or to see the end beyond the sacrifice!

If this describes you (and/or someone you know), allow this power-packed book to serve as YOUR personal guide, helping you to **<u>Confront Your Comfort and Excel in Your Press</u>***! Get ready to introspectively identify the root of your stagnation, via thought provoking written exercises, prayer, and biblical meditation. It is my personal prayer that the eyes of your understanding would be enlightened, that you may know the hope of God's calling on your life...that you will not only gain* *the insight and strategies necessary to push past every obstacle, but you will be fully engaged and find excitement in finally exiting that cycle of self-sabotage that is hindering you from achieving your vision.*

If you are anything like me, the last thing you want is to grow old and realize that you never grew up. Nor do you want to get to the end of your life holding onto purpose that is unfulfilled. So, allow your investment in this book to ignite or reignite your developmental process...let it be the beginning of an elevated belief in your ability to succeed in every area of your life. There is **VICTORY IN YOUR VISION** *my friend and there is a multitude of people waiting for you to manifest yours, in order to experience the victory that's in theirs. I'm looking forward to your testimony!*

~ Shannon

Shannon T. White, MSW, LCSW, Mindset Coach

INTRODUCTION

How many times do storms or challenges come along in your life, causing you to fall off the "vision bandwagon"? You are persistently heading towards your destiny and gung-ho about the plan. Then, with no warning in sight, the roadblocks of distraction, anxiety, and fear appear dead smack in the middle of the lane! They cause you to reroute and take a detour or even teeter and tumble clear off the wagon into the land of self-sabotage and inaction.

I presume you wonder why it is so easy to get off track. Well, quite frankly **there is simplicity in faltering when we lack understanding about the intricacy of our purpose**! Most of us don't even realize **_why_** we are here or the impact of carrying out the vision that God has given us for our lives. As a result, it doesn't take much to push us into fear, interrupt our peace and/or knock us off course, altogether.

My intention is to provide you with an overview of the mindset shift that needs to occur if you want to avoid mental chaos, move beyond your comfort zone, and press your way into your victorious place. I encourage you to take your time with each chapter and thoughtfully respond to every question and thought-provoking exercise. It is also recommended that you take some time RIGHT NOW to pray and ask God for His wisdom before you read any further. This will ensure that your ears are open for each applicable point that He intends for you to internalize and act on, as He stretches you beyond your limited area of comfort and pushes you into the vision that He has given you for your life.

And just in case you struggle with praying on your own and are more at ease allowing someone else to pray, I will give you a one-time pass to get you started. However, the buck stops here! God is stretching you, so get ready to press beyond your comfort zone! By the end of this book there will be no more excuses for immobility in ANY areas of your life. Reaching your victorious place is ultimately up to you and you will be equipped with the preliminary tools to get you in position for just that! So, take a moment to ask God (in faith) to elevate your trust in His will for your life and to increase your capacity to **confront your comfort**, so you can ultimately **excel in your press**! And don't be afraid to declare this prayer out loud, with a spirit of boldness. God will meet you at your level of expectation!

Shannon T. White, MSW, LCSW, Mindset Coach

Father God, I come before you with a pure and open heart, ready to hear and receive from you as I read this book. I declare that every chapter and every exercise will benefit me, totally increasing my understanding of your will for my life. I no longer want to remain in a place of mediocrity, so Lord I welcome the stretch that will move me into the next best version of myself. I am ready to hear from you and grow in your wisdom, so that I can become all that you created me to be and do all that you have predestined me to do. Thank you, in advance, for increasing my trust in your willingness and ability to deliver me COMPLETELY from fear, anxiety, pride, self-doubt, lack, procrastination, dormancy, ignorance, negative thinking, chaotic situations and anything else standing in the way of my predesigned, victorious life. My ears are open to you, Lord. I stand ready and willing to do the internal work required to be stretched beyond the limited area of my comfort and catapulted into the vastness of my purpose. Thank you for every test, trial and sacrifice that you have used and will use to develop me, Lord! Thank you for choosing and preparing me for such a time as this! Thank you for giving me the tools necessary to carry out your perfect will and purpose for my life. Thank you for clarity concerning my vision for it is that clarity that will be the guide to my victorious place!

In Jesus' name I pray, Amen!

As your first act of faith, I encourage you to very intentionally meditate on any parts of this prayer that resonated with your spirit. Then, pull out a highlighter and <u>highlight</u> those parts for future reference. Also feel free to <u>take notes of your thoughts</u> in the space provided on the next page. The process of change will take a lot of intentionality and a heart of expectation.

Are you ready for the press? Let's go!

Shannon T. White, MSW, LCSW, Mindset Coach

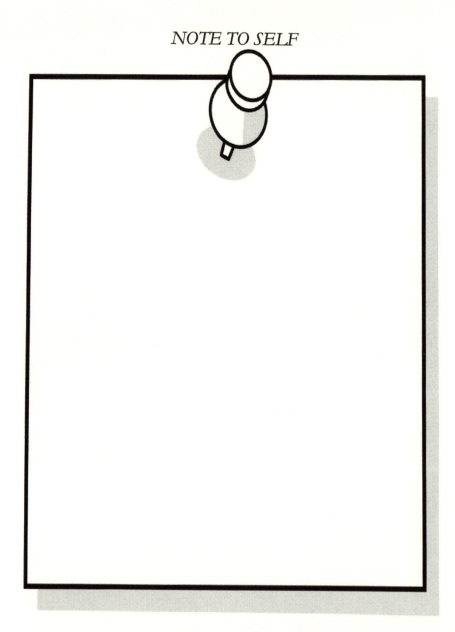

1 THE CHALLENGE

Your best friend calls you one winter afternoon, asking you to make a commitment to go to the gym with her four days per week at 5:30 am. You immediately scream, "No Way!" She proceeds to quickly remind you of your New Year Resolution to work out more frequently and recaps the part of that conversation when you promised to be her accountability partner in achieving the same goal. You literally cringe at the thought of waking that early and enduring the physical pain of an undesirable workout. You can honestly care less about that unreasonable resolution because frankly you didn't believe you could follow through anyway. After all, you have never been successful at maintaining a work-out routine for more than a couple days at a time in the past. However, you reluctantly say "yes", out of a sense of obligation to the friendship and the commitment you made.

Every other morning, the dreadful sound of your alarm and the nauseating dinging of the three snooze alerts, wake you up cursing your friend. You pray for an extra 10 minutes of sleep as you pull the blanket back over your head and enjoy the warmth of your bed. Before you can nestle back into your heavenly slumber, she sends you her giddy, "I'm a morning person," reminder text and you dreadfully pull yourself out of the bed, stomp through your dark bedroom and begrudgingly put on your tennis shoes and work-out clothes.

Each off night before bed, you pray for the morning text to read, "I can't make it to the gym today". But low and behold, morning arrives, and the happy reminder text arrives for three weeks straight…ugghhh! Mornings are getting colder as the winter chill sets in, but you continue to go through the same morning routine until that providential day when the million-dollar text comes through. "I can't make it to the gym this morning…not feeling well. Enjoy your workout!"

Music to your ears! You find yourself quietly rejoicing, so you don't wake the rest of the house and, with a smile on your face, you climb back into bed. Your body could care less about your mind's sheer confusion. This is your deciding moment! Do you push past the discomfort of getting out of that comfy bed and press your way to the gym without your friend or does your body convince your mind that one day off won't hurt?

Somewhere in the plethora of your thoughts of everything that you have to do today that requires a well- rested body, you consider getting up. But as easily as the little voice of reason stumbles to the forefront of your mind, your self-talk even more effortlessly pushes it back into your subconscious and directs the course of your actions. You decide to sleep in and ignore the prompting, since there is no real power to that internal urge anyway. For the next two days, your friend is sick, and you succumb to the warmth of your cozy bed.

Like most of us who lack inner conviction, you fail to realize that one conscious decision or one action step has the power to change your whole trajectory in that short moment! Here is the problem. In all the early morning work outs, you never found the inner drive to realign your thoughts and push your body past the pain and discomfort. Your main focus, outside of your sore muscles, was an <u>external</u> obligation to please your friend. So, when you didn't have to please her anymore you chose inaction. In order to build the mental muscle necessary to push past the physical pain, there needs to be something that <u>internally</u> convinces you to keep going, in addition to the outward benefits of those crunches and leg presses. In fact, I am willing to argue that building mental muscle is the ONLY way to successfully push past the pain and to stop believing self-defeating thoughts (i.e. I can't take it; I don't feel like it; It hurts too much; I don't think I am capable; I am too tired to get up; I have never been good at sticking to my workouts).

Maybe you didn't educate yourself enough on the long-term benefits of a healthy lifestyle or weren't convinced by your best friend's testimony of how she achieved her 6-pack abs, firm glutes and toned legs. Is it possible that you have bought into the "I just can't do it" lie or that your healthy living, weight loss or body toning goals seem way too far off? Perhaps you've been bitten by the instant gratification bug, so you cannot accept that every inch eventually adds up to a mile… especially since you still can't fit last year's jeans and your stomach is hanging over your pants even as you are reading this!

Regardless of whether your struggle is with working out, weight-loss, shopping too much, road rage, unforgiveness, yelling at your children, poor relationship choices, procrastination, lack of motivation, inconsistency or all of the above and more; there is a very simple and achievable plan to move from settling in the mediocre to living a life that exudes victory in every area. It is totally about learning to build that mental muscle I mentioned, through a reviving and renewing of your mind. It is focused on developing an unshakeable inner motivation that gives you the stamina to stick with the plan and push past the discomfort. It is what you become, by finishing, that makes every part of the journey and every sacrifice worth it.

If you are like me, you have tried everything from prayer, to fasting, to guilt and possibly condemnation. You have blamed your inaction on stress, your family, your neighborhood, your job, your dog, your past and even God. Therefore, I am here to convince you that both the answers to your lack of progress and the willingness to change truly rests within you! Research indicates that a person is more likely to change poor habits or consistently work at and complete a task if they are internally motivated, as opposed to externally obligated. The good news is, no matter how many times you have failed in the past, there is nothing that can stop you from reaching your goal if you so CHOOSE to do the internal work first.

Now, if I still have your attention, then you have an inclination that you are the hindrance to your own success; however, you realize that you require a plan that doesn't rely on an obligation to meet the needs of someone else. The question is, are you ready to do the internal work to make an external change? Here we are, back at that deciding moment! Will you pull the covers over your head and remain settled in your comfort, or will you push past the pain and allow a little discomfort to change your life forever and for the best.

We all reach that moment in life where we desperately want to figure things out on our own and we are convinced that our experiences have equipped us to do things differently next time. But I am here to tell you that without the God-given steps laid out in this book, you will find yourself on repeat playing the same "Woe is Me" soundtrack. For the next few chapters, allow this book to be your guide for confronting your comfort. If you are willing to do the work, the light bulb of your mind will ignite, helping you to work past your fears, eliminate self-defeating thoughts and excel in your press! Now, if you are not convinced that you need help, you can certainly put this book down. But mark my words, your old routine WILL inevitably creep up on you again and again…you will repeatedly find yourself climbing back in that bed! So, let's get started….*Are you ready for the challenge? Are you ready to expose yourself to the chill and move beyond the coziness of that comfortable place?*

"The Master, God, opened my ears, and I didn't go back to sleep, didn't pull the covers back over my head" Isaiah 50:5 (MSG)

Applicable Action Point

*1.) Maybe your struggle is not with working out, but the truth is we all "**pull the covers over our head**" at some point or another during our life journey, often prolonging our trip to victory. Take a moment to write down the areas of your life where you know you have been perpetually "pulling the covers over your head and falling back asleep", as opposed to getting up and taking action. This is the beginning of understanding your purpose (or what I refer to as your **WHY**).*

2.) What purpose does pulling the cover over your head serve?

3.) How has pulling the cover over your head prolonged your journey to your victorious place? How has it stopped you from living out your dreams or the vision that God has given you for your life?

2 THE WHY FACTOR

Intentionality is often the face of change and a very necessary step to developing internal motivation. In fact, everything that is successful in life starts with an intention or a determination to act or behave in a certain way! An intention implies a little more than what you may be "thinking of doing" or "considering". It is more so **the outcome of what you decide to set your attention on; your actual <u>reason</u> or <u>purpose</u> for doing something.** Intention is your *why*. So, what's your intention? In other words, how do you define your *why*?

If you are anything like me, that is a daunting question. It is one that seems pretty simple on the surface but requires great thought and consideration. If you are truly honest with yourself, answering that question can be quite intimidating! However, knowing your *why* is by far the most crucial weapon you can have and is necessary for the win in every test and battle in your life. Your internal motivation naturally builds once you begin to determine your intention for doing something. Therefore, knowing your *why* will make it harder to pull those covers over your head, as we discussed in Chapter One.

Like millions of other wives/mothers, I used to think my *why* was my husband and children. Everything I set my attention on led directly to caring for and showing my love for them. In actuality, though, I was minimizing my *why* and only identifying with one part of it, based on some very limiting core beliefs. Because of my own experiences and upbringing (not being raised by my own biological parents who were teenage parents that never married) it was comfortable labeling my husband and children as my reason for working hard, enduring pressure, building my business, taking care of my health, living "right", *etc*. I was determined that I would break the cycle for my own family. After all, that is what society says a good "wife" and "mom" focuses her attention on and what my core beliefs and perceived expectations about parenting and marriage caused me to believe. It honestly made my *why* kind of "easy" to explain and comfortable to live in.

I was about three years old when my biological mother met my stepfather and almost five when they had my first younger brother Shawn. Two years later they had my brother, Sterling, and about 6 years after that, my little sister. Unfortunately, their struggles with addiction and domestic violence interfered with child-rearing, causing all four of us to grow up very quickly. Because I had a different biological father than my siblings, I spent a lot of time with my maternal and paternal grandparents. I bounced back and forth between my mom and stepfather's house and my grandparents' houses, until I permanently moved in with my maternal grandparents in the 3rd or 4th grade. My paternal grandmother was instrumental in taking on the caretaker responsibilities of my biological father (who really was not emotionally or physically present in my childhood years), and she selflessly shared the job with my maternal grandparents. I tell you this not to shame my bio-parents who were only 17 years old and babies themselves when they conceived me, nor my stepfather who I believe truly loved me like I was his own, but to provide a backdrop of where a lot of my insecurities, internal struggles, and core beliefs and values derived.

By the age of 12, I had gotten my first job. I spent a lot of my paycheck and the money from my child support checks that my father sent, making sure that I had the things I wanted when my grandparents couldn't afford it. The remainder was used for my younger siblings. I always worried about what they needed, so I did what I could to make sure they had what I perceived as "enough" gifts on holidays and "enough" clothes at the start of the school year.

As early as the age of five, I can remember making bottles for my, then, newborn brother Shawn. I babysat, changed diapers and cared for him just as if he was my very own. In my mind, I was his protector and by the time he was 14 years old, I was literally his provider. After my freshman year in college, I got full custody of Shawn and raised him until he turned 18. A little over a year after I graduated from college, I became the guardian of my then 16-year-old brother, Sterling. So yes, I have literally been raising or helping to take care of my family since I was 5 years old (sounds unbelievable right)! As a result, I was always beyond my years when it came to demonstrating responsibility for others. In fact, I spent a great deal of my life thinking God created me primarily to parent and care for others. Unfortunately, both of my brothers were brutally murdered (Sterling in 2006 and Shawn in 2008), which is a devastating story that I will save for another time.

It was these tragic losses that began to open my eyes to the idea that ***my why had to be bigger than the box I had so neatly fit it in***. By the time I mentally arrived at the place where I could honestly begin to process my grief, I was already married to my amazing husband, had given birth to my four wonderful children and had a rewarding career. However, regardless of the accolades I received for being such a "strong woman", "good wife", "great mom", etc. (despite all that I had been through), I was living with a wealth of confusion about the true nature of my ***why***.

I asked myself a question that no parent or wife ever wants to consider... What if tomorrow comes and my children or husband, like my brothers, are no longer around? In that scenario, what would become of my ***why***? Would my ***why*** or the purpose of my existence come to a screeching halt? Is being a wife/mom or having the "perfect" little family all God created me for?

It was in that moment that I realized there had to be more. However, I had no idea how to define myself, nor my very existence outside of being a mom, wife and a nurturer. And, in order to be those things, I **had** to be STRONG. Those labels validated me. My childhood parentification defined me. I started to examine the core beliefs that led me to a very limited perspective of what I was designed to set my attention on. And, I was blessed to conclude that I was not created just to be a wife and mom. Instead, being a wife and mom are two of the many assignments attached to my purpose. In other words, these roles, albeit extremely valued and important, are not the **totality** of my *why*. Do not misunderstand what I am saying. My husband and children are definitely my first ministry and priority, after God; however, there is a larger overarching reason for my existence on this earth which I will get back to in a bit. Hang in there.

"My why had to be bigger than the box I had so neatly fit it in"

In the meantime, let's take an inventory of the steps necessary to identify your intention or the purpose of your existence (your *why*). Then, we will dig a little deeper in the next few chapters, examining the sacrifices it will take and the beliefs and vision you will need to successfully carry out your *why*. During this journey, you **will be challenged** to confront your comfort. You **will be pressed** to take a more in-depth look at the core beliefs and the "safe places" that limit your thinking and tell you that your *why* is not attainable. Furthermore, you **will be encouraged** to use the gift of your imagination to develop a preview of the life God truly has for you, and to create the structure you will need to arrive at your victorious place. Hopefully, you can handle the stretch because there is no more time for delay. Your time for change is NOW!

WHY: THE OUTCOME OF WHAT YOU DECIDE TO SET YOUR ATTENTION ON; YOUR ACTUAL <u>REASON</u> OR <u>PURPOSE</u> FOR DOING SOMETHING.

Applicable Action Point

1.) Take a moment to reflect on your own story. In reading chapter two, was there anything specific, either from my story or the ideas outlined in the chapter that resonated with you? Free write what comes to mind, prior to moving on to the next chapter. Really take some intentional time to tell your story... at least the beginning!

Continue to tell your story here…

*2.) I mentioned earlier that loss helped me realize that my why was bigger than the box of wife, mom, and caretaker I put it in. Now that you have had a moment of self-reflection, what box do you think you have so neatly fit your **why** into?*

3 IDENTIFYING YOUR WHY

*T*he Webster Dictionary defines the word **why** as *"for what cause, reason or purpose"*. Other sources define **why** as *"the reason for which something is done"*. The degree to which you identify and define your **why**, is the degree to which you will begin to attract and achieve the success or ***victory that lies within your vision***! It is your **why** that will determine where your attention needs to be focused, earnestly showing you the areas of your life that are out of balance and prohibiting forward movement. I will take it a step further and argue that *it is the black and white definition of your why that makes focus possible and your vision clear.* It is that definition which helps you press on the challenging days and forces you not to give up even when the stretch seems too much to bear.

Your **why** should pinpoint the reason or purpose for which you were created. It should be your sense of resolve or determination, outlining specific gifts, duties, requirements or assignments (*i.e.* being a great spouse, raising your children, starting that business, standing up for that cause, obtaining your degree, working out, committing to a healthy lifestyle, *etc.*) that may require sacrifice, but will always circle back to your ***why***.

My spiritual father, Bishop John Edmondson, once mentioned how silly it is to buy a luxury car and never read the manual to find out all the intricate details and great features of the high-priced vehicle. That analogy stuck with me and developed in me a firm belief that if you want to know the purpose, or ***why***, of something or how it is supposed to properly work, you must study the manual. In other words, look to the manufacturer for the intent of the original design. With that being said, in order to truly identify your own personal ***why***, you must be willing to study the manual that comes from the ultimate manufacturer…the Creator God, himself!

Now, it would be presumptuous of me to think that everyone reading this book consistently reads or totally trusts in the manual that I am referring to, and that I consider the absolute truth governing my life. And, that's okay because everyone is entitled to their opinion. However, I challenge you to stay open-minded and keep reading anyway. You might just find some jewels and, better yet, some answers about your ***why*** in the promises from the Bible (the life manual I am referring to) that I plan to share with you.

Let's start with these words from David in the book of Psalm 139:13-16 (NIV). *"For you created my inmost being; you knit me together in my mother's womb. I praise you because I am fearfully and wonderfully made; your works are wonderful, I know that full well. My frame was not hidden from you when I was made in the secret place, when I was woven together in the depths of the earth. Your eyes saw my unformed body; all the days ordained for me were written in your book before one of them came to be".*

And then, there are the beautiful words of Jeremiah in Jeremiah 1:4-5 (NIV) that read, *"The word of the Lord came to me, saying, 'Before I formed you in the womb I knew you, before you were born I set you apart; I appointed you as a prophet to the nations.'"* For those of you who are thinking, 'what do David and Jeremiah have to do with me', consider Acts 10:34 that tells us "God is no respecter of persons." I submit to you that the word of the Lord that came to Jeremiah holds true for me (Shannon), just as much as it holds true for you (insert your name). **"Before I formed you in the womb (Shannon) I knew you, before you were born, I set you apart; I appointed you…"**. Hear me when I tell you, God doesn't favor David over Jeremiah, nor me over you. He sees us ALL as his perfect creations that <u>He set apart to fulfill something very specific; whose days have already been written and whose steps have already been ordered</u>. That means no matter your current position or the level of comfort or confusion you are in right now, God wonderfully made you for an appointed purpose, a very clear *why*!

If you don't mind, I just want to dwell here for a moment, so forgive me if I sound repetitive. However, I need for you to really sit in these scriptures for a moment in order to develop a mental picture of the process of your creation. Consider the fact that it truly doesn't matter what everyone sees when they look at you, what circumstances you may have been conceived under, or what bloodline you were born into because the one who created you (our heavenly Father God) designed you in secret. He **INTRICATELY** weaved you together (piece by piece) and set you apart for greatness. He made absolutely no mistakes and every part of your being was made specific for your design (even before you were thought of by your mother and father... even before you were conceived). So, consider that if God took this much time with you, He just might have the answers to identifying your overall *why*!

> Definition of **Intricate**- with many parts; artfully combined; containing many details or small parts that are combined in a particularly complex or skillful way (Encarta Dictionary)

In fact, I **know** He has the answers. One of my absolute favorite scriptures, Jeremiah 29:11 (NIV), reads, *"For I know the plans I have for you," declares the Lord, "plans to prosper you and not to harm you, plans to give you hope and a future."* The word "plan" is defined in a few different ways...as a detailed proposal for doing something or achieving something; an intention or decision about what one is going to do; a detailed blueprint or diagram. So, my friend, the Lord is saying that your life is already mapped out, detail by precious detail, and that a future designed to prosper you is your expected end! Isn't that good news?! All you need is a vision of that life and an internal motivation to pull it from within and walk it out. This internal motivation will develop as you feed on the truths of God and walk in harmony with those truths (James 1:22; John 13:17).

God has set you up to experience WHOLE life prosperity. And, He promises that as your soul prospers, everything else (physically, mentally, financially, etc.), will follow. It is your spiritual prosperity that will provide you the wisdom to excel in every other area, allowing you to carry out your special responsibility or appointed purpose (your *why*) in the world. Believe it or not, there is a specific group of people and a special set of circumstances that are eagerly awaiting your obedience to release what God placed on the inside of you.

> "Beloved, I pray that in every way you may succeed *and* prosper and be in good health [physically], just as [I know] your soul prospers [spiritually]"
> - 3 John 2

I know this may sound scary and you may even be asking yourself how. However, in the planning stages of your life God was thoughtful enough to provide you with every tool you will need along the way. You can rest assured that you are FULLY equipped for the task at hand. In His strategic plan for your purpose, God provided you with both natural talents and spiritual gifts that are essentially the tools you will use to accomplish your *why*. Your main job is to be a good steward over those specific gifts and talents, according to 1 Peter 4:10. They are intended to be used for the service of others in God's overall plan for this world, which I submit is key to understanding your specific *why*.

Your gifts and talents essentially undergird your *why*. While they may look or present differently than mine or the next person's, everyone's individual gifts and talents function as a piece of God's overall puzzle. So, from a corporate perspective, we actually multiply one another's power when we all understand the individual part that we play. This means that my *why* will never be as impactful alone, as it will be if you do your part for God and operate in your *why* too. Understanding your individual role (your *why*) in God's bigger picture will give you clarity about the road to your victorious place (or whole life prosperity). It will also show you how to use your gifts and talents to exhibit God's truth amongst the people that He has specifically assigned to you.

In short, identifying your *why* creates somewhat of a chain reaction that begins with your act of obedience to:

(1) Tap into the gift that is already inside of you,
(2) Examine your discontent regarding your current position in life,
(3) Rely on and maintain an attachment to the gift-giver (the Creator) for direction during your course, and
(4) Serve those divinely assigned to you, so they might be able to identify and assume responsibility for their own *why*.

Ultimately, when all is said and done, identifying your *why* opens the door for the words, "Well done, thou good and faithful servant" (Matthew 25:21 KJV), to be spoken to you by God.

"It is the black and white definition of your why that makes focus possible and your vision clear"
- Shannon White, Mindset Coach

Applicable Action Point

1.) First, list your natural talents? Then, based on 1 Corinthians 12:7-11, what do you believe are your spiritual gifts? (Note: you have at least one spiritual gift...<u>no one is left out</u>!)

2.) How are you using these gifts currently to glorify God?

> 1 Peter 4:10 (ESV)
>
> ¹⁰ As each has received a gift, use it to serve one another, as good stewards of God's varied grace"

3.) **Read and reflect** *on Paul's words in 2 Timothy 2:2 (NLT): "You have heard me teach things that have been confirmed by many reliable witnesses. Now teach these truths to other trustworthy people who will be able to pass them on to others"*

How would you LIKE to use your gifts/talents to better glorify God and pass His truths on to those people that have been divinely assigned to your purpose?

4.) *Now, I want you to go a bit deeper! Take a moment and attempt to identify and define your why. (Note:* **You will have an opportunity to come back and tweak this, if necessary, later**. *Just reflect on your* current *intention(s) and write down what comes to mind). Here are some questions to ask yourself:*

- A) What is **your** overall intention for your life or intention for what you are doing in this season of your life?
- B) What do you see when you envision your future?
- C) What is it all about? Who is it all for?
- D) What will ultimately determine if you are victorious?
- E) How do your gifts and talents undergird your why?

...Continue brainstorming your *why* here. Remember, you can always come back and tweak this later!

> The Webster dictionary defines the word why as "for what cause, reason or purpose". Other sources define why as "the reason for which something is done".

5.) Say a prayer asking God for discernment and understanding, then re-read and jot down the words/phrases from Psalm 139:13-16, Jeremiah 1:4-5, Acts 10:34 and Jeremiah 29:11 that really stood out for you. In your own words define what those words/phrases mean to you personally and why they registered with your spirit.

6.) How do the words/phrases that resonated with you in #5, line up with your response from #4?

*7.) In what ways do you think gaining clarity about your **why** might help you stay on path to see God's vision for your life come to pass and help you reach your victorious place?*

*8.) Lastly, make a **<u>daily commitment</u>** to pray over your gift(s) and your individual role in the kingdom of God. Ask God (the giver of the gift) for your specific delivery system in getting your gift out to the world or carrying out your why (Remember **it is your gift/talent that undergirds your why**).*

4 MY TESTIMONY…THE ROAD TO MY WHY

You know, God has more than likely been giving you glimpses of your *why* for a very long time. I was reminded of my many glimpses when I finally got serious and obedient about writing this book. I picked up some of my old journals and realized that although the discovery of my *why* began a very long time ago, the revelation of the black and white definition of my *why* started in 2010. I had begun to attend services at Victory in Christ Christian Center, the church where my spiritual father, Bishop John Edmondson, pastors. On July 4, 2010, Bishop challenged the congregation to begin to seek God for our purpose (our *why*). We were given the assignment to read and meditate on Ephesians 1:18 for a week straight, asking God for revelation. Bishop assured us that God would begin to give us dreams and visions, illustrating our purpose.

The eyes of your understanding being enlightened; that ye may know what is the hope of His calling, and what the riches of the glory of His inheritance in the saints- Ephesians 1:18 KJV

I will be honest. I was skeptical, but at the same time curious. You see, I had gotten to a place of feeling desperate that there had to be more to my life. To recap, I had lost my two brothers by this time. Although I was going through the motions and appeared physically strong from the outside, I believe now that I was emotionally breaking on the inside. Despite having a beautiful, healthy family and a great career, I felt dissatisfied and discontent. There was something stirring on the inside of me, telling me there was more. I had been earnestly praying and believing God for more.

To nudge me further, my mind kept replaying the words of the keynote speaker of an event I attended on my 33rd birthday, 4/14/10. This event was just a couple months prior to the assignment given at Victory and during, what appeared to be, a very dry season of my life where I had many questions for God about why things didn't seem to be "working". The speaker looked me in the eyes and specifically said, "every word that comes out of your mouth will come to pass. You will be known by name. You will live a life of prosperity". She then finished by saying, "God says, 'I hear you. I only want to prosper you'", as the choir sang a song that repeated the words "just love, trust, and obey". I was on a spiritual high from that promise for only a few days before thoughts of doubt, uncertainty and fear began to creep in.

In the back of my mind, mental pictures of my past began to play. I started to wonder how God could possibly use me. I was a product of a teenage pregnancy, witness to parental drug/alcohol addiction and domestic violence, and a victim of emotional neglect and abandonment. There was an underlying fear of failure that sometimes prevented me from moving outside of my comfort zone, or "safe space", and other times motivated me to overcompensate and chase unnecessary avenues of perceived success.

Clearly, my outward appearance didn't match my inner struggle. Internally, I felt like I was carelessly tossed to the side by those who were supposed to love me most as a child; thus, my self-esteem was certainly impacted. As a teenager, I was mean, angry, hard-headed and an emotional bully and grew up to be a very resentful, judgmental young adult. My tongue was so sharp it could cut ice and my words so harsh they could crush someone's whole spirit. I searched for love in all the wrong places and settled for toxic relationships and unhealthy intimacy well into young adulthood. On the outside, I was clothed in a false sense of strength and confidence and on the inside the unresolved trauma and painful past was slowly breaking me down. I was holding tightly to this façade, but definitely feeling the pressure and losing my grip. I knew I needed to deal with myself, but the truth was much too painful.

So again, how could God use me knowing all of this? Better yet, why would He choose to use me in such a huge way? I always knew I was different and had "something to do in this world", but my inner critic and the voices of all those people who said my poor attitude would stop me "from doing anything" rang very loudly in my mind for many years; thereby, minimizing my **belief** in "what I could actually do". By that point, I had accepted Christ as Lord and Savior and had begun to develop a personal relationship with Him as my God. I was fully aware of my authority as His child, believed He forgave me for all my shortcomings, and understood that I was and am capable of doing all things through His strength. However, I was not totally convinced that the speaker's message would ever come to pass given my flaws, nor that God actually meant for the message to be delivered to me.

But, isn't God gracious? Isn't He good for confirming his message to me just a few months later? One morning, after I was given the assignment to read Ephesians 1:18 and diligently seek God for my purpose, I was in the shower and had a very clear vision of a glimpse of me carrying it out. I will be honest, the platform and the impact that I had in this vision was so large that it frightened me. Without going into all the details, I was speaking over the lives of a great multitude of people and they were attentively listening. They had come to hear me speak and even passersby were stopping to listen. The looks on their faces told me that whatever I was saying was impactful and changing their perspective. I know that may sound crazy to some people reading this, but God didn't stop there. He followed that up by giving me the following scriptural reference (in case I needed more clarity about my *why*), with a very intentional and <u>specific action step</u> leading to my victorious place:

*"The Lord God hath given me **the tongue of the learned**, that I should know how **to speak a word in season to him that is weary**: he **wakeneth morning by morning**, he wakeneth mine ear **to hear as the learned**"* -Isaiah 50:4 KJV

As I previously mentioned, this was just the beginning of God revealing the specificity of His purpose for my life. It was also the beginning of my awareness of the gifts that He placed on the inside of me, that would ultimately serve as a catalyst to the manifestation of my *why*. In my work with many influential people, I have found that the very thing they struggle with most (*i.e.* areas of inconsistency, behaviors that others point out as a weakness) is simply their gift, *perverted* (definition: having been corrupted or distorted from its original course, meaning, or state). The bitterness and dwarfed confidence that I possessed as a child due to my upbringing, directly led to my hard exterior, harsh words, poor attitude and lack of vulnerability. However, it also built resiliency, an ability to persevere and a desire to exhort hope. My childhood parentification allowed me to develop great leadership and teaching skills. I was quick and witty with my words (even though they sometimes hurt people), which translated well into my gift of creative writing and public speaking. As the nurturer that I was, I can remember secretly trying to help even my enemies. I often encouraged others that were in some way struggling (when I wasn't using that creativity and their vulnerabilities to break them down).

The change that occurred from the girl I was to the woman I am becoming (and I say becoming because I am still a work in progress), began when I made a conscious decision to pray for my purpose and to gain an understanding about ways my gifts could be used in carrying out my purpose. I also decided to literally attach myself to God (the creator and gift-giver), so I hear directly from him, rely less on my own strength and distorted defense mechanisms and more on His insurmountable power and sufficient grace. I realized that I often abused my gifts of wit and creativity to "tell people off" verbally or in writing. Furthermore, I used my gifts of encouragement and nurturing to subconsciously gain emotional validation in areas where I felt void.

While I received that prophecy in 2010, I would be a liar if I said that I spent the next decade consistently walking in love, trusting in God's plan and obeying His every instruction. Nor did I wake up "morning by morning" so I could attentively hear from God. I told you before, I am hard-headed and, to keep it even more real, I have been known to procrastinate from time to time (I am literally laughing out loud as I type, because I can picture those who personally know me giggling hysterically at the understatement of that last sentence). However, I have learned that God is faithful and strategic. He only gives us glimpses of the overall vision to ensure our long-term success in achieving it. His delivery method allows us ample time to mature, so we do not squander our gift. Thus, every sacrifice and setback, during the journey, is simply a setup for our success.

I have personally learned to never despise the process and to willingly allow myself to be molded by my experiences. It is in the pull that God is preparing and stretching me for the vastness of my purpose, or my *why*. Even in the many glimpses of my *why* that God has given me over the years, I would have been totally unprepared to carry out the totality of the victory He began to define for me back in 2010. It has literally taken each and every one of the small incidents, changes and sacrifices to get me to my current place and guess what… I still have not totally arrived. Habakkuk 2:3 (ESV) says "For the vision awaits its appointed time; it hastens to the end- it will not lie. If it seems slow, wait for it; it will surely come; it will not delay."

Sometimes we get anxious and move too fast in the course of trying to find the victory that lies within our vision. We take shortcuts and neglect to build the foundation because we want to see the end without the pain of the process and without the discomfort of every aching step. Unfortunately, we end up causing more of a delay most of the time. Frankly, it is always easier to sit comfortably in a state of inaction or to rush through the movement. We must be very careful, for rushing the process can actually destroy us if we are unable to manage the goal. Furthermore, sitting still in a state of inaction means that we will miss the goal altogether. We must take an active listening position with God. The more I heed the instruction I was given to spend time listening to God's voice "morning by morning" and the more I love, trust and obey, the more my mindset is aligned and the more the vision is activated.

I often think of this rainy morning, after I mustered up the courage to step out on faith and start my own business. I was driving to a networking breakfast at a Cracker Barrel Restaurant just a few towns from my home. I highly anticipated the event for weeks prior, knowing that some of the industry's most successful entrepreneurs would be in the room. I was told that it was "the place to be" for entrepreneurs just getting started in business. I looked forward to learning how to introduce my business with a "30- second commercial" and could barely wait to swap my freshly printed business cards with potential referral sources. And let's be honest, I really looked forward to the pancakes I could almost taste on the drive over.

Anyone who has children knows the importance of properly preparing the night before if you need to be anywhere by 8:30 am the next day. Despite that inner voice that pleaded with me to do so, I had failed to plan, thinking I could "wing it" since the restaurant was only about 25 minutes away. Afterall, I didn't need to be there at exactly 8:30...guests would only be mingling at that time. I didn't plan for delays, I didn't lay the kids' nor my attire out the night before, I didn't prepare their lunches for school or daycare and, on top of all that, I failed to gas the car (so I had to stop at the gas station in the morning). Of course, everything that could go wrong that morning DID and by the time I got ready to get on the road to travel to my destination, it was already 8:15. I put the address in my GPS, as I tried to maintain a positive attitude, and said out loud "a few minutes late won't hurt." I put my right blinker on, heading towards the highway, but the GPS directed me to go left towards some back roads that (in my brain) would take at least 10 minutes longer on a normal, non-rainy day. Thus, I decided to take the highway instead.

I clearly remember the GPS repeating its direction for me to make a U-turn towards the back roads, but I did my own thing and took another right onto the highway. I drove about a quarter of a mile and ***BAM*!!!!!** I came to a screeching halt after running dead-smack into bumper-to-bumper traffic. At that point, I started to panic, shaking my left leg franticly and stretching my neck as far as I could to try to see the road ahead. With no exit in sight, I angrily inched my way up the road for another 2 miles. I looked at the clock and realized that I still had about 23 miles to go and it was already 8:40 am. My body tensed up and I started to convince myself that I would never make it at a decent time. I did what any "sensible" person would have done…began planning my big escape off the northbound route to go back home.

As my vehicle slowly crept up to the next exit, I got a feeling that I should just keep going towards my destination. At the same time, I got the "wise" idea that I should take that exit and drive another route that I had traveled in the past. All I cared about was finding a shortcut to bypass the traffic. So, I again ignored the GPS as it told me to make a U-turn to get back on the highway. I remember smiling, thinking I was smarter than the GPS, as I drove traffic free. After a while, the GPS began to get the hint that I wasn't going to turn around and it re-routed, giving me instructions to go in another direction that just didn't make sense in my mind. I had traveled this way many times before, so I kept driving the "shorter", familiar route despite the persistent instructions of the GPS. Before you knew it, I ran right into traffic again. I could almost feel my blood boiling in anger, as I approached a stoplight. The GPS told me to make a left turn into what looked like even more traffic. To be totally transparent, I was pissed by this point, so I snatched the GPS off my dashboard, threw it on the passenger seat and yelled "shut up, I am going straight!". This tantrum was followed by the following emotionally charged plea, as I banged my hand on the steering wheel, "GOD WHY IS THIS HAPPENING?!!" No sooner than that question exited my mouth, I looked over to the left and there was a car approaching with one of those Jesus fish license plates. Right away, I heard a very calm, still voice in my spirit, "are you going to keep trying to take short cuts or are you going to follow My instructions?"

You see, that's what I love about our Father in heaven! He is never moved by our emotional outbursts, nor does He leave or take a time out from us when we plan our own course. Like any good parent allowing their child room for growth, independence and development of adaptable ego functioning and critical thinking skills, God will allow us space to see what works and what doesn't. Similar to that GPS, He will provide step-by-step directions before our journey when we request His help. He will even give us multiple prompts to redirect our path when we get off course, but He will not force us to turn back when we continue to go in the opposite direction, despite His instruction. He will stick out the ride with us though, always right there offering to lead the way when we get tired of going in our own direction.

Needless to say, I made that left, bypassed any further traffic and was at the Cracker Barrel in less than fifteen minutes. As a result of my failure to follow instructions, I missed the 30- second commercials in the beginning, but I still had time to swap business cards with potential referral sources and was able to enjoy the succulent taste of those Cracker Barrel pancakes.

There were times in that situation, and other similar situations, that I mentally wrestled with condemning myself about the opportunities I missed due to my late arrival. It is probable that some connections that would have been forged, had I listened to the GPS and avoided my perceived "shortcuts", were missed. However, I now know that the ones that were truly for me were not forfeited. I believe that my God is so good that He used that experience and many others to expose me to myself.

Obviously, there were still some unusable components of my character that I needed to address (*i.e.* lack of preparation, comfortability with lateness, control, pride, disobedience, etc.) in order to prepare me for the next steps of the vision and all the doors I would be walking through in the next few years. That experience wasn't really about the 30- second commercial, connections, nor the pancakes. Instead, I believe it was to change my perspective from a place of external motivation to internal dedication in the pursuit of my ***why***.

It has taken a lot of wrong turns, pitstops, backtracking and internal battles for me to finally reach a place in life where my motivation is no longer driven by external factors. While those factors may play a part in getting me to think about the changes that need to be made, the real motivation is based on an internal desire to stop the mental chaos; or the incongruence in thoughts that has served as a super unhealthy part of my comfort zone for a very long time. Both, the assignment that God has placed on my life and the vision that He is continuing to unfold, echo much too loudly in my mind to just sit idle. In fact, the mental chaos I had become accustomed to no longer overrides my deep-rooted need for mental alignment.

In other words, **my comfort zone became very uncomfortable**; thus, change was inevitable. I came to a point where I truly wanted to experience the peace that I desired, and the fulfillment promised by living out my *why*. Therefore, I had to take some very intentional action steps to get to where I am currently, and I will continue to press to get to where I am going. I have embraced the process and likewise, I encourage you to do the same!

I would like to help you break down Proverbs 13:12, as you consider the idea that owning your journey (or your process), is just as important as experiencing the victory associated with reaching the destination. Every test, trial and let down thoroughly prepares you for where you are headed. The beginning of Proverbs 13:12 says, "Hope deferred makes the heart sick, **but**...." Now, keeping in mind that the word "but" signifies the entrance of a contrasting thought, this scripture should actually excite you (despite how it starts). The preceding comma gives you permission to pause or to breath, while the conjunction "but" prepares you mentally for something totally opposite of that dismal beginning.

Therefore, before giving up during the setbacks of your journey, ask yourself how you can use those pauses as setups for your outcome. Because I am a sucker for celebratory endings, I will go ahead and give you the rest of Proverbs 13:12. It reads, "...but desire fulfilled is a tree of life." My friend, this is saying that even through the detours and waiting, you can go ahead and shout with joy about the abundance of life destined to spring forth on the opposite side.

"Hope deferred makes the heart sick, but desire fulfilled is a tree of life"- Proverbs 13:12 NASB

Applicable Action Point

*1.) What glimpse(s) of your **why** do you recall receiving, even at an early age?*

*2.) In Proverbs 18:21, the bible says that "life and death are in the power of the tongue...". What words have been spoken over your life by yourself or another person, that have either limited or excelled your ability to walk in your purpose, or your **why**?*

3.) In what ways have you taken shortcuts and even neglected to build the foundation, because you were too impatient to wait for what came after the "but" that is mentioned in Proverbs 13:12?

4.) How have these shortcuts and/or lack of foundation impacted your success or movement toward your victorious place? What have they revealed about your character?

*5.) Describe your level of **external motivation** versus **internal dedication** to pursuing your **why**, based off of these last few chapters of self-reflection?*

5 OUTLINING YOUR DAILY ACTIONS

Every day you are capable of moving one step closer to your victorious place. However, you must be willing to take some bold, deliberate steps forward. I will warn you that these steps may require sacrifices and risks that cost you your comfort and force you to push past where you are currently. Most people are unwilling to press towards their vision and become who they were created to be because they are too attached to who they have been and what they have been accustomed to doing. However, once you have clearly defined your *why*, your thoughts and actions must follow suit if you truly desire to reach your victorious place.

If your *why* is living a long and healthy life so you can educate the world on how to conquer some life limiting disease, then every action you take should line up with that *why*! You will see that the family health history (external factor) that may have started your desire to change is no longer your primary driving force and getting up in the morning to work out is no longer based on your friend's participation. You must become internally motivated by the inner belief that working out is a necessary step to living a long healthy life. In other words, your *why* must be powerful enough to outweigh your perceived problems (*i.e.* that annoying alarm clock, winter morning chill, the aching of your muscles, etc.) and cause you to think **and** act in alignment with your ultimate vision.

Soon you will see that you won't even give thought to your family medical history because that becomes a tactic to keep you bound in fear and anxiety. Instead, you will be moved to carry out your long-term, God-given purpose. You will begin to set your attention on your intention(s) and after a while your daily actions will naturally include healthy lifestyle changes and other things that develop a strong sense of health consciousness because it is now something you value... something that is genuinely important to you.

At some point in my personal journey, I realized an incongruence between my values/beliefs and my behaviors. Because of the way I grew up, I developed a scarcity mindset that caused me to *believe* that I had to "hustle" and work as many jobs as possible to achieve my goals, obtain degrees/certifications to determine my success and hold on to my money to ensure that I was never "broke". Now promise that you won't judge me, but I would actually do things like pay a minimal, partial payment on a bill (even when I had the whole amount in the bank) just so my account would not be empty. I was literally holding on to what God blessed me to pay the bills with, while accruing interest and extending/ doubling balances...just digging myself deeper into debt because of fear.

Since my childhood was pretty limited in these areas, I *valued* time with family, giving to others, quality things, pleasing God and making beautiful memories. I always had the idea that my children would never **want** for anything, they would have the **best** of everything, and would travel and be exposed to **ALL** the "finer things". I was witty and quick on my feet, so I very quickly found myself becoming the jack of all trades, yet the master of none. I worked as many jobs and side hustles as I could fit into a day but missed valuable time with my family while doing it. I developed very poor money management habits and distorted ideas about money that pushed me further into the lack from my childhood that was created by generations of family members before me. Ultimately, the very things that I was trying to avoid exposing my own children to (debt and the continuation of financial strain) became my reality. I realized very quickly that I was living in an illusion of success, built on the shaky foundation of a poverty mindset.

There was an obvious contradiction between my values, beliefs and behaviors and it wasn't until I decided to shift from the many jobs to my **why** that I realized just how incongruent things were. You see, the hustling that I was doing to earn a paycheck, holding two to three jobs at a time, allowed me to focus only on the surface needs of the people I was serving. I knew how to perform most of my job duties without even thinking, which made working multiple jobs easy. However, I soon realized that I had begun to almost prostitute my God-given gifts, talents, skills and abilities to the highest bidder. My primary motivation was externally driven by my earnings for the week. Thus, my relationship with work assignments eventually began to lack substance and ultimately became very transactional. I certainly was not indebted to any of my side jobs and, had a better financial opportunity come along, I definitely would have moved on to the next best thing.

Although I was good at a lot of things, I was even better at compensating in the areas that I had not yet mastered. Therefore, I didn't have to stretch much or think a lot to get my assignments done. I simply had to sacrifice my time and some of my sanity because of the amount of stress I was undergoing to keep up with my many unnecessary assignments. Eventually, though, all of the long hours and late nights negatively affected my family; limited my ability to walk in my authentic purpose; and hindered my impact on those I know I have been called by God to influence. I was afraid of being broke and complacent with being unfulfilled, so my natural actions were, at times, contradictory to my God-given purpose and values.

I determined that change required a commitment to transform my thinking, particularly about money and success. I began to reflect on my values, or my deeply held beliefs, discarding the ones that I saw as negotiable and honing-in on those that are more so non-negotiable. When I say "negotiable", I am referring to those things I am not committed to sacrificing for. I realized very quickly that there are three distinct values that I am, however, willing to sacrifice for. Each of them is rooted in a place of love and I have discovered that *whatever we love we will sacrifice for*. Maybe that is why God gave me the message to "love, trust and obey" so many years ago.

I essentially began to re-evaluate and redefine my values, as I thought more pragmatically about my *why*. I found that my desire to follow God and His plan (and one day hear Him say, "good and faithful servant, job well done"), my desire to live prosperously in EVERY area of my life (spiritually, emotionally, physically, and financially) and my desire to leave an impressionable legacy for my children that will lead to positive generational impact, are the values that internally motivate me to operate in my *why*. It was these and others like these that began to identify me personally and differentiate me professionally from others in my industry. These values are now embodied in my day-to-day interactions and decision-making; and are further exemplified in every professional program, product and service that I offer, as I strive towards the vision of motivating and helping to change the mindset of those who may otherwise have difficulty doing it themselves.

The challenge to my success and to anyone's success, is usually the level of commitment to our sacrifice. In other words, how much is it worth to you? Are you willing to risk it all? To what degree are you willing to press past your discomfort for the values you say you hold dear (despite the difficulty of the task)? How much are you willing to invest? Which old habits, relationships, fleshly emotions, maladaptive thoughts, etc. must you eliminate from your life in order to truly excel in your press towards your victorious place?

When I was just starting out in my career as a therapist many, many years ago, I was introduced to a concept for the process of change. I do not take credit for it and despite my research, I have never been able to determine the originator of the concept. However, it made such an impression on me that I have adapted and used it in my professional and personal life ever since. The concept is based around the mathematical symbol of change, the delta (Δ), and it basically says:

Investment + Responsibility + Accountability =
Change

A good visual of the concept is as follows:

I.R.A. = CHANGE!

If you want to see a positive change in any investment, you must consider the level of sacrifice you are willing to make. Let me make this plain for you. If you deposit a mere $10 per pay period into a retirement account, then your return on investment will be a lot less significant in the long run than if you sacrifice $100 every pay period. You must ask yourself, when you are making your payroll deduction elections, "Just how much do I love the idea of financial freedom when I am no longer able to work?" While it may hurt to lose that extra money on a biweekly basis, especially if you are already living paycheck to paycheck, envision the joy of having an income to fall back on while you are home relaxing after retirement.

The road to your victorious place requires a very similar mindset as it relates to the equation of change. You must be willing to make an **investment** in the process, knowing that your ultimate success will depend on the level of sacrifice you are willing to make, the risks you are willing to take, or the degree to which you value the change you would like to see. There will be certain **responsibilities** that come with that, such as spending time with God for direction, consistency, persistence, renewal of your mind, thought shifting, elimination of dead ideas and emotions, repositioning of unhealthy relationships, etc. And finally, you must get to a place of taking full **accountability** for your progress, or lack thereof. Determining that there will be no more excuses and accepting that you can no longer blame your past, your present or the people in your life for your lack of movement, is the piece of the problem that will complete the equation.

You see, I could not totally follow God's plan if I were unwilling to make a total investment in the process, heed to my responsibilities, and take accountability for the part I play in God's overall vision for my life. I could no longer be selfish with my resources, ideas, talents or gifts, nor squander them in areas that didn't require me to grow or stretch. I truly had to become a good steward over everything that God has given and continues to give me, no matter how difficult it sometimes is to do so. Furthermore, I had to be willing to take the sacrificial steps God was requiring of me to not only find myself, but also increase my capacity and change the trajectory of my thinking.

Everyone's steps will be different, but the key is ensuring that your daily actions follow the vision of your *why* which God has given you. For me, the key components to carrying out my *why* were transformative in nature, changing me from the inside out. I was specifically instructed to rise early (Isaiah 50:4) every day, in order to be in God's presence.

The purpose of my early rising is to ensure uninterrupted, intimate time worshipping, praying and meditating on the word of God. This time with God allows my thinking to align with my Creator's, so my self-talk mirrors His voice. I was also challenged to love others even when I didn't think it was deserved, to trust God even when it seemed impossible, and to obey Him even when I thought my route made more sense. In making the effort to submit in those areas, God began to reveal every other corresponding, strategic action step that will ultimately draw me closer to the vision (my victorious place).

I can clearly remember the many prayers in which I pleaded with God to show me why my business wasn't prospering at the speed in which I thought it should be. Afterall, I had made the commitment to give up my many jobs and focus on my *why*. There were several times that I heard the answer in my spirit. However, I wasn't ready to come out of my comfort zone, challenge my learned behaviors and habits, nor do the work that God required of me in order to gain the victory. I had clarity that, according to Proverbs 18:16, my gifts would put me in situations and in front of people who God has divinely aligned with my purpose. I kept hearing, in the spirit, that my provision would only come when I trusted God's instruction to first <u>build the foundation</u> and <u>develop my gifts</u>. This ensured that I would be prepared for those open doors and opportunities. But you guessed it! I was hard-headed and focused more on immediate financial return.

Instead of developing the ideas and programs that I knew God was telling me to sacrifice my time and immediate financial gain for, I would default to things that required less brain power. I would think of some t-shirt design or e-book that I could whip up quickly to make an extra twenty dollars. While an extra twenty dollars may have put more in the bank immediately, I was still hustling harder than I needed only to maintain a continuous cycle of lack that was built on the poor financial habits and learned behaviors of my past. However, shifting my thinking allowed me to see that working towards my vision by developing those God-inspired programs and ideas will ultimately give me ownership to the means to create long-term wealth. I can remember a season where literally every witty, "hustle- spirited" idea seemed to dry up, as I insisted on doing things my own way. I now believe that it was God's way of helping His "hard-headed" child find the balance I had become accustomed to living without.

In that season, I came to the realization that I could no longer focus primarily on the financial increase, if I wanted to reach my victorious place. I had to first renew my thinking and develop spiritually in order to rise from the comfort of that poverty mindset. Without spiritual development, I was emotionally inept and physically drained and would remain financially overdrawn. There had to be balance if I desired whole life prosperity. As I became more spiritually aware, I also received the following revelation: my desire to leave an impressionable legacy for generations to come is not determined by how much money I have. It is determined instead by how much impact I make on those depending on me to live out my purpose and serve them with my gifts (1 Peter 4:10). And I honestly believe that any successful entrepreneur or *why* driven person, living out the call God placed on their life, would agree.

"God has given each of you a gift from his great variety of spiritual gifts. Use them well to serve one another"- 1 Peter 4:10 NLT

Applicable Action Point

1.) Let's start by examining your values. Your values are the things you believe are most important. They help to determine life priorities, and they influence decision-making. For example, if you value wealth you might prioritize your career, however, if you value family, you might try to spend more time at home. Free of judgment, take a moment to list your values on the chart below.

The values *I'd like to live by*…	The values I *ACTUALLY* live by:

2.) *List some of your core beliefs and their origin. How did your beliefs help to shape your values in life?*

3.) *When your actions do not match your beliefs and/or values (e.g. valuing family, but working a lot), you may become discontent. Is there any incongruence between your beliefs and/or values and your actions? Write your thoughts here:*

4.) *Now go back and revisit your **WHY** from the Applicable Action Step you wrote out in Chapter 3. Is the meaning behind your **WHY** powerful enough to naturally move you to act? Do you care enough about it to push past the comfort of those cozy covers? Are you willing to **invest** enough, even to sacrifice in areas that may be painful?*

*If your answer is not a strong, confident **YES**, then take a moment to examine the values and beliefs that undergird your perceived **why** and redefine it accordingly based on the vision that you know God has given you for your life. Now, ignore all negative thoughts telling you it's not possible; and rewrite your **WHY** here...after all, you have a legacy to build:*

5.) *Next, take a moment to make a bulleted list of the steps/actions you think you need to take in the next 90 days or the **responsibilities** you know you have in carrying out your **why** on a daily basis. If you are a goal-oriented thinker, you can think of this list as short-term objectives to carry out your long-term goal/purpose--your **why**). **NOTE**: I'm not looking for perfection here, just a list of your thoughts about what you think it will take to totally operate in your **why** in the next few months.*

-
-
-
-
-
-
-

6.) *Finally, let's get rid of all your excuses!! What areas have you been neglecting to take total **accountability** for, in your change process?*

Now let's recap the last few chapters and please allow me to be very direct in my questioning.
- Does your *why* line up with your core beliefs and values?
- Does your *why* outweigh the magnitude of your perceived problems?
- Can you change your perspective to see that "early morning workout" (or whatever else you are facing) as a small steppingstone on a huge mountain that you are aggressively climbing to reach optimal health or your ultimate *why*?
- Are you truly convinced that you can do this, or are you worried or fearful that you won't have the stamina to endure the fight?

If you are more inclined to lean towards the latter, you are perfectly normal and ready for the next chapter. After all, **success in reaching your victorious place is a process**. By sacrificing your time and submitting to the process you are giving God the ability to build and develop you. Sure, God could simply deliver you from what is prohibiting you to move forward, but in the process of growth, it is the discomfort of the process that helps you to thirst after and internalize life-long change and total dependence on Him. It is what you become after finishing this book (and every other life test and challenge), that makes the sacrifice worth it!

Use the space on the next page to free write as you think about and answer these "re-cap" questions. It is important to be honest with yourself, remembering that ***if you expect*** *change, the only one responsible for your success is YOU!*

6 *THE CHOICE*

Here is the thing...EVERYONE has been given the gift of FREE WILL. In other words, God's will for our life is not automatic, nor will He ever force you to do what you do not want to do. You have essentially made a choice about your outcome in every life transition and decision-making moment of your existence. If you take a second to think about your failures and your successes, you will realize that there was a moment of deliberation that moved you in the direction of your end result. You either chose to do it or you chose not to. In many instances, your decision or indecision to move was rooted in some life experience and the emotion that experience created for you in the past. Or, it is based on your level of comfort with what you desire now, as opposed to what you desire most.

I submit to you that the decision to stretch beyond your perceived capacity, as opposed to you doing what is comfortable, is one that requires an unshakeable faith or the confidence that you can achieve something that appears to exceed your human ability. Hence, your victory in every challenge ultimately lies in your belief in the "impossible" and willingness to do the corresponding work. Hebrews 11:6 (KJV) tells us that "without faith, it is impossible to please Him... He is a rewarder of them that diligently seek Him." So, when you exhibit a faith mindset, while conscientiously seeking an understanding of **God's** plan and principles for your life, you can always expect success. However, I am fully aware that certain life experiences may have hindered your full capacity to believe.

Experience usually supersedes every other influence in your life. So, it is natural to focus more on where you are and the evidence that you have right in front of you, than it is to focus on an *"idea"* of where you should be or what it seems you are unequipped to accomplish. Once you develop a perceived "truth" about your situation, it is very difficult for your conscious mind to change that belief or move beyond the limited scope of what you can physically see. Thus, it is normal to stick with your habitual response and return to your comfortable place of being (even when it hasn't gotten you very far in the past and may have gotten you off task on more than one occasion). People generally learn by association. Thus, your subconscious, automatic response system kicks in when a stimulus reminds you of some past experience, and resumes functioning at the level that your subconscious mind has locked into. Your "free will" becomes almost limited, as a result, because your subconscious mind autopilots you back into your safe zone. In other words, it is human nature that you default to your comfort zone.

The only way to correct your subconscious response is to change your conscious thoughts, including your perception, thoughts, and feelings about the stimulus. The ability to do this requires you to think beyond the limited scope of your own perspective. You will also need to have faith in and renew your mind with God's truths concerning your life and your circumstances. And finally, you must commit yourself to changing the words that come out of your mouth (Proverbs 16:23). We will discuss this more in the next couple of chapters, but first let's look at how your default thinking has developed over time.

The human belief system is predicated on 4 major influences that I want you to think about as they relate to the decisions you have made:
1. Your **environment** of reference
2. The **people you are in relationship with** or those you see as reliable or trustworthy in your life
3. The **information** you constantly hear
4. Your **experiences** (which we already determined trumps everything else)

Identifying what drives your belief system is the key to changing your outcome. You will have what you believe and say in life. Thus, it will first be necessary to gain a clearer perspective of what shaped the thoughts leading to what you believe you are capable of doing or achieving. Once you have identified the underlying reasons for your thoughts, you can begin to change your words to line up with the truth of God (outlined in the manual of life—the Bible) and then start boldly speaking over your situation to reprogram your beliefs.

Your Environment

The neighborhood, state or country you grew up in, the schools and religious institutions you attended, your workplace, your social location (i.e. social class and gender) and your current environment all serve as agents of socialization. They work together to shape the way you see and respond to the world around you throughout the course of your life. Here are some examples to help you better understand this sociological phenomenon:

- If you grew up in a low-income neighborhood where most families struggled to make ends meet, you might also possess a "poverty" mindset. When it comes to decisions about finances, saving money might be difficult, paying bills on time might seem foreign and thinking small might seem safe, regardless of your current economic situation.

- If you have lived all your life in a community that is made up of predominately one racial group and/or socio-economic class of people, then you might not believe you can adjust to an environment where the majority does not resemble you. You may also be more prone to prejudge or stereotype people who are different from you, finding it difficult to accept and include people of different backgrounds.

Therefore, your environment plays a huge part in the development of your norms, values, attitudes and behaviors. Even as your environment changes over the course of your life, you will typically hold onto thoughts and feelings associated with your place of reference when shaping your decisions.

Relationships/Credible People
The first group that has a major impact on who you become is your family of origin (the family who raised you); however, as you grow you also develop relationships with a variety of people and friends along the way. There are certain individuals (whether related or not) that you come across, whose beliefs, behaviors, values, thoughts, ideas, etc., somehow resonate with yours or whose vision you find value or truth in. These are the people you most often view as credible and who have the most influence in shaping the way you see life.

Many times, it is the credible people in your circle that help you identify your sense of self, develop ideas about who you are, and determine what you deserve out of life. Insofar as the direction that my professional life has taken, there are many people whose ideas and beliefs resonated with me, far before I totally understood God's vision for my life. They range from high school counselors, to college deans/professors and motivational speakers like Les Brown. However, I want to spend some time telling you a little bit about the two most influential people in the development of my core values and beliefs. Trust me, their influence could be a whole separate book, but I will just share with you some things that changed my *"forever"* and made me so passionate about vision and purpose. It is truly this part of my story that helps me to realize the truth in the promise God provides in Romans 8:28 which reads, "a*nd we know that God causes* *everything to* **work together for the good of those who love** *God and are called according to his purpose".*

Despite my upbringing, which in retrospect was a very necessary part of my process, God gifted me with the love and nurturing of my maternal (Roberta) and paternal (Viola) grandmothers from birth to adulthood. They were the ones to plant the seeds of hope, forgiveness and strength, as well as my work ethic and drive to excel beyond my circumstances. I can honestly say that without my grandmothers, I probably would not be the woman that I am. Like every human being in the world, they had their faults, but even those God worked together for my good.

Grandmom Bert specifically taught me the valuable lessons about God, marriage, motherhood, and education that I carry with me until this day. She was married to my grandfather for over 50 years (one of the only long-term, committed marriages that I was ever exposed to as a child). Together, they raised 13 children of their own and then selflessly accepted the responsibility of raising my cousin and me. The dignity and virtuosity she modeled while rising early to take care of home, her husband, her children, and the responsibility of her domestic jobs outside of the home, was the closest example I have of the Proverbs 31 woman I am still striving to be. Most importantly, Grandmom Bert instilled the habit of studying my bible and telling others about God very early on. She made sure that my education was primary in my development, so my dreams would never be deferred.

Grandmom Vi was also instrumental in my faith development. It was her strength and her independence, as well as her no-nonsense attitude that helped to nurture my resilience, tenacity and genuine freedom in Christ. She taught me by her actions that the enemy had NO POWER over me as a child of God. It was actually her testimony of forgiveness that got me through the murders of my two brothers. When I was about three years old, my biological father's 15-year-old sister (Grandmom Vi's only daughter) was brutally gang raped. She died about a week later due to the injuries sustained from the attack. When I was about seven or eight years old, I can remember my grandmother and I driving down the road in her town and seeing a man walking. My grandmother waved and said hello. After we passed him, she told me that he had been one of the suspects in my aunt's unsolved rape and murder.

I will never forget the rage I felt. You see even though I was so young when my aunt passed, God gifted me with very vivid memories of her spending time with me. I loved when she would take me to the park and push me on the swings. I remember her smile and the way she used to look at me. I also remember her peaceful, yet cold body in the casket and then never seeing her again outside of those other beautiful memories. But most of all, I remember the pain and emptiness in my grandmother's eyes in her brief moments of silence. So, for her to say hello baffled me. But her response was one that carried me when I was later given the responsibility of speaking on behalf of my family at the sentencing of my brother Shawn's murderer.

That day, Grandmom Vi told me that our Father in heaven was the only one capable of judging the sins of man. As a result, she knew that God would deal with each of the men who had a hand in my aunt's death in His own way and in

His own time. She had to forgive, not so much for my aunt's murderers, but so that the pain of the loss would not control her or take her out of right standing with God. There were still many other lives that Grandmom Vi knew she was responsible for impacting. I realize now that my grandmother understood the very premise of living in her *why*. She missed her daughter every day, but unforgiveness and hate would never allow her the freedom to live victoriously. Remaining in a place of pain would simply prohibit her purpose. You see, her calling did not end because my aunt's life did. She had to keep going.

I literally watched my grandmother walk in that strength following the impact of many important losses, from her own husband, her mother, her sister and her sister-in-law (who was more importantly Grandmom Vi's best friend). However, that conversation in her car truly stuck with me most, building my foundation for forgiveness, resiliency through loss and trust in the Lord. I never saw her skip a beat either. She just kept pressing towards her victorious place, until the day she transitioned home to be with the Lord.

I truly thank God for allowing me to recall, feel and identify the emotions of those memories because in His divine, omniscient way He knew that I would one day need them to carry me through one of the most difficult days of my life. No one but God can get the glory for what I am about to share with you next because most of it was a total blur. I do not know how the words formulated in my mouth and flowed so eloquently, nor do I understand how I never broke down. I was able to walk in that courtroom on December 8, 2011, look my brother Shawn's murderers in their eyes and tell them that I forgave them. And to this day, I still mean it. I miss Shawn tremendously and my family will NEVER be the same. However, the vivid memories I have of my aunt, made my grandmother's forgiving response a permanent imprint in my mind. Between that and the strength of both my grandmothers, I was impacted in a way that shaped my attitude. I developed a total trust in God's ability to bring peace, despite my family's devastating loss.

After praying and asking God to allow me to be a mouthpiece for Him, I declared that God would get the glory and lives would be saved. What came out of my mouth next was something that I believe the Father Himself needed those men to hear Him say. I don't know if it was something that they had never heard before or something that they needed to be reminded of. All I know is that in my human flesh, those words could not have been my own. I told them that although Shawn's purpose was prematurely aborted due to their careless actions, they would still have a life to live and people to impact with their own gifts and testimony after their (minimal, in my mind) twelve- year sentence.

Despite my devastation about losing Shawn only two years after losing my brother, Sterling (two of the first human beings that God gave me the gift of nurturing), I believed like Grandmom Vi that the pain was not about me and that God was the only One who could judge. I hadn't realized it until then, but I had begun to rest in the familiarity of unresolved grief, that I was still carrying from Sterling's unsolved murder in 2006. I never had "closure" (as if there is such a thing) after Sterling's murder, so in many ways, an unconscious hate had begun to stifle my ability to walk in my purpose. Joy would only come if I released the burden of unforgiveness. So, with the help of God's grace (His empowering presence), I was able to confidently tell those young men that God STILL loves them both and that they STILL have a purpose to live out. My prayer was, and to this day continues to be, that they would repent for their sins, accept the Lord into their heart and identify their *why* while serving their sentence. I prayed that God would show them His vision for their lives, so they too can live out their purpose and not take it to the grave prematurely.

Repetitive Information

According to the American Psychological Association, a child sees an average of 40,000 commercials in a year. This indicates that, by the time most people are in their senior years (65 and older), they will have watched millions of commercials. The messages that you repetitiously hear through the mass media, school, religion, family, credible people in your life, etc. is also a huge source of your ability to believe or not believe. In fact, companies spend millions of dollars on advertising because they know that the more you hear or see a message, the more you will believe it. Discipline is rooted in repetition, so in that same respect, our minds are disciplined to think a certain way based on what we hear over and over again. Eventually, thoughts become so much a part of our subconscious mind that the only way to change those thoughts is to plant some other message at the forefront of our imagination.

Joshua 1:8 (NLT) says to *"Study this Book of Instruction continually. Meditate on it day and night so you will be sure to obey everything written in it. Only then will you prosper and succeed in all you do."* According to the Oxford Dictionary, the word meditate is defined as to "think deeply or carefully about something." We often think more deeply or more comfortably about the messages that are commonly heard in our environments, our experiences and from the credible people in our lives. This is why it is so easy to develop a subconscious comfort in dwelling in stagnant and mentally unhealthy places.

However, when we renew our minds daily by reading God's word and we educate ourselves with His promises and plans for our lives, we gain new information to replace those negative thoughts. Then, when we pray (which is simply talking to God, thanking Him for who He is to us, making petition for the manifestation of His promises and/or repeating the word of God through our declarations), as instructed in 1 Thessalonians 5:17, we begin to see the change that we are believing for, take root. Slowly, we are reprogramming our subconscious thoughts, until they become our automatic conscious thoughts. Even when old thoughts try to infiltrate, which we will discuss in the next chapter, we are able to successfully negate them and continue to press forward.

Experiences
It is our experiences with the various agents of socialization, that I mentioned previously, that truly shape our mindset. You have likely heard the phrase, "it's not what you say, it's how you make a person feel". Well that concept is what makes experiences so powerful. Your

experiences are made up not only of the feelings surrounding the incidents, but also mental pictures that get stored in your subconscious and words that accompany those images, just as I described the emptiness in my grandmother's eyes in her moments of silence after losing my aunt. As a result, each life experience leaves a permanent imprint, even when you cannot consciously remember the exact details of the incident. As early as childhood, our experiences lay down our basic foundation in life; however, there is good news. We are not obligated to keep these orientations to life unless we choose to. It is all about that deciding moment and the free will you have to choose how you want to see your life play out.

The question is how do your choices lead you to, or misdirect you from, the place God called you to be? How much do your experiences, your environment, the repetitious information you have received, or the people you have in your inner circle influence your decisions? Would your decisions be different if you found more value in where you are headed or more discontent in where you started? Take a moment to think about these questions. Then, complete the following applicable action point. **Reflect** on your most recent major life decision, **based on the four influences** I just described.

The key is to be as honest as possible, so you can gain a visual representation of the many thoughts (rational and irrational) that go through your mind when you are in the process of operating in your free will. Once you face your own perceived truth, I want you to take a look at God's truth. This will preface your understanding of why you often remain immobilized in what you WANT, despite what you know you NEED to do.

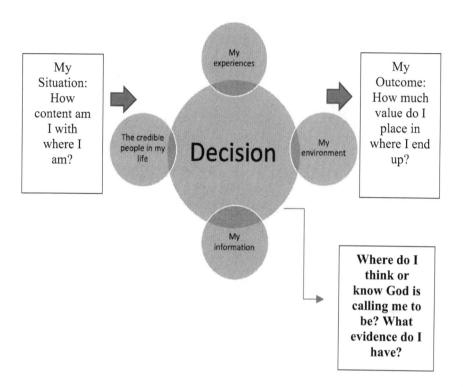

This is usually the time when I provide you with a word of inspiration or a bible verse before going into the applicable action points for each chapter. However, I feel led to share the scriptural confirmation that God gave me the morning after I made the choice to stretch beyond my comfort zone, believe God, and allow myself to be led by His presence in that court room. You can read it word for word on your own, but here are the highlights of Philippians 1:20-30 that stood out for me during my intimate time of prayer and study with God that next morning. Go ahead and read the passage of scripture in whatever translation of the bible that you best understand; however, I suggest that you meditate on it in the Message version of the bible, just so it can truly hit you like it hit me.

Phil 1:18-25 MSG (highlights of the passage as spoken by the Apostle Paul):
"So how am I to respond? I've decided that I really don't care about their motives, whether mixed, bad, or indifferent... I know how it's going to turn out. Through your faithful prayers and the generous response of the Spirit of Jesus Christ, everything he wants to do in and through me will be done. I can hardly wait to continue on my course...everything happening to me...only serves to make Christ more accurately known, regardless of whether I live or die. They didn't shut me up; they gave me a pulpit! Alive, I'm Christ's messenger; dead, I'm his bounty. Life versus EVEN MORE life! I CAN'T LOSE."

Now I don't know how reading that made you feel, but even as I typed it, I felt like jumping out of my seat and celebrating!!!! So, in the next set of questions, I want you to take some time to reflect on the choices you have made or need to make in order to stretch beyond your perceived capacity. Take your time and identify the influences hindering your ability to believe. Again, your victory in every challenge ultimately lies in your belief in the "impossible" and willingness to do the corresponding work. Are you ready to do the work?

> ***Applicable Action Point-** Be totally honest!*

1.) The decision I need/needed to make in order to stretch beyond my perceived capacity:

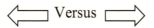

2.) What did my environment, directly or indirectly, teach me about handling this situation or making this decision?

3.) Who are the people I look up to, or whose ideas/positions do I respect? How might they handle this decision?

4.) What information or messages have I repetitively heard or been hearing about this particular choice (pros and cons, good/bad, etc.)?

5.) What is my current mindset about the choice given my past experiences?

6.) On a scale of 1-10 (1 being not comfortable at all & 10 being extremely comfortable), where is my comfort level with my current state of being and/or doing? Which specific factors caused me to choose that rating?

7.) Where do I want to end up? How do I want this chapter of my story to end?

8.) What is God saying about the choice I have? What is my scriptural evidence of His position/truth?

Note: *If you are unfamiliar with specific bible verses regarding the topical area of your decision, feel free to use a search engine such as netbible.org to complete your part of this applicable action point.*

7 THE POWER OF YOUR MIND

In order to develop in your ability to make choices that truly follow God's lead and embody the authentic you that God created you to be, there is a constant mental battle that you will have to fight. As a child of God, recognize that you have an enemy whose primary measure of success is keeping you from living the life of victory you were predestined to live. The moment you try to expand your territory and walk in your purpose, he will show up to accuse, deceive and tempt you.

> *Be alert and of sober mind. Your enemy the devil prowls around like a roaring lion looking for someone to devour.*
> **1 Peter 5:8** (NIV).

The enemy sends uninvited mental visitors to overhaul your conscious thoughts and maintain your subconscious level of comfort. Such things as distortion, lust, self-doubt, fear, etc. come along to govern your mindset and devour any semblance of confidence or clarity about your purpose that you may have. If the enemy can successfully use his schemes and lies to get your thinking out of alignment with God's promises for your life, defeat is much more likely. This is why he starts attacking your mind as early as you are able to develop memories. If he can cloud your thinking with his lies, he knows your authentic, true nature may never come to the surface to live out God's vision for your life.

This is why it is so important to identify your authentic self and become content with your *why*, or the God-given purpose for which you were created. When you operate from that place of wisdom and faith, you leave no room for the fiery darts that the enemy throws (Ephesians 6:16) to create detours on the path to your victorious place. This is the first step to building your mental muscle. Every excuse and self-defeating thought that causes you to pull those covers over your head and ultimately restrict your growth is exposed when you gain understanding of who you are. I also submit that it is your knowledge of self that aids in the correction of flaws in your mindset.

There are three components to your mindset that the enemy is after in his attempt to minimize your territory and diminish your influence. In order for you to defeat the enemy and reach your victorious place, your beliefs; thoughts; and actions must all align. Because you are reading this book, I can almost bet that this is exactly where you are being attacked and where you are more than likely struggling to find harmony. So, let's take some time to define them individually and gain a good understanding of the part each component plays in achieving the victory.

Beliefs and the Subconscious Mind
Your subconscious mind, the part of the brain that is under the surface, takes care of most of your basic life functions. The subconscious is the location of your brain that

activates your fight or flight response when you are in danger or when you need to react quickly. It exposes your learned behaviors and habits whenever you have to make decisions. And, it is where your experiences, knowledge, and beliefs are recorded and stored. Most importantly, as it relates to your victorious place, your subconscious mind is where your vision is incubated. Truly your subconscious mind is the powerhouse of your brain, controlling about 95%-97% of all your behaviors and reactions.

Your inner motivation dwells in your subconscious mind, as does the origination of your actions and your belief system. I would particularly like to draw your attention to beliefs as they relate to the subconscious mind and reaching your victorious place. Beliefs can be likened to your voice of reason. The problem is, when you have limited knowledge of your authentic "made in the image of God" self (which is also housed deep down on the inside of your subconscious mind), your voice of reason can be tainted by that historical foundation of life experiences that we discussed in chapter six. As a result, whatever you have learned to be real and true within that subconscious context will suffocate your authentic self and come out in your conscious thoughts. It will also fuel your action or inaction. You don't even have to think about these things most of the time, because they literally function on autopilot or become second nature (your comfort zone). This is why your conscious mind is so important.

Thoughts and the Conscious Mind
I tend to think that God was very thoughtful when He created the human brain. It seems that His intention was to

ensure that the brain operated as efficiently as possible to cause His children the least amount of stress. In order to fully function, the brain requires a great deal of energy. So, the reason so much processing occurs in the subconscious mind, is to give the conscious mind a break. Even though the conscious mind is only responsible for the other 3%-5% of your behaviors and reactions, the level of thinking is more immediate and complex at the conscious level. In fact, your active thoughts are a **conscious** culmination of your perceptions, feelings, will, intellect, desires, personality and those subconscious beliefs we just discussed. Now, I don't know about you, but just reading all of that is enough to make a person tired.

The conscious is, what I like to call, "the forefront of your imagination". It works to provide a safety net for your learned behaviors and habits, whether healthy or maladaptive, and often uses irrational thoughts to justify your current level of functioning. Unfortunately, thoughts are flighty. They change frequently based on the situation and despite your beliefs. Therefore, if you are not mindful and in control of what you think, feel, or do; your conscious mind can cause mental chaos.

Your conscious mind also has the power to either birth or abort the vision that is incubating in your subconscious. Even when you "know" and believe your purpose deep down in your core, the enemy will send such infiltrators as: doubt, pride, distortion, misperception, worry, fear, anxiety, depression, anger, unforgiveness, hostility, jealousy, guilt, shame and a host of other unwanted mental visitors. They are notorious for bullying your "know better" and they serve to rationalize unhelpful and/or negative behaviors. They literally take residence in the conscious part of your brain and will revisit as frequently as they desire, until YOU learn to take control and command these uninvited visitors to leave. They are well aware of the incongruent relationship that exists between your conscious thoughts and subconscious beliefs. But they patiently wait for an open door that they can access to bogart their way in. Thus, you must be constantly working to renew your thoughts if you want to achieve your goals.

Actions -also known as- External Behaviors
Finally, you have your actions, also known as your external behaviors. Your actions are fueled by both your thoughts and beliefs. However, I submit to you that real consistency in your actions is a manifestation of what you subconsciously believe. If you don't really <u>believe</u> you have the capacity to maintain consistency in working towards your *why*, your actions will exhibit just that. Despite even your most convincing thoughts, you will find it difficult (if not impossible) to take the appropriate action, if you have not yet developed a new belief system that internally motivates you to do so. You might have a temporary change in your behaviors, based on what you think that change should look like; however, as soon as your thoughts are infiltrated or you feel discomfort, you will very quickly resort to your comfort zone again.

Beliefs + Thoughts + Actions = Mindset

If you review the challenge in chapter one, you will see that you never really believed that you could follow through on your New Year Resolution anyway, based on failed past attempts. Although you felt externally obligated to work out when your friend was going to the gym with you, you never found the internal motivation to realign your thoughts and push past the pain, when the external factor was gone. You were beginning to develop a pattern of working out, which would have eventually changed your subconscious experience and created a new norm, but that pattern was interrupted much too soon to see a lasting change. Therefore, it was simple for you to stay in your comfort zone, or the warmth of your bed.

You will very quickly find yourself in a terrible cycle of inaction, inconsistency, or maladaptive behaviors until you find alignment between your actions, thoughts, and beliefs. Unfortunately, if you don't subconsciously believe in your capability to do something, it won't take much to throw you off course. The only solution is to develop a new mental habit, or stronger mental muscle. Developing a resolve to create a new habit/experience and taking the necessary action steps will be the only hope for replacing old beliefs that dwell in the subconscious mind.

"For as he thinks within himself, so is he" - Proverbs 23:7 NASB

Applicable Action Point- *Reflection Time*

Take a moment to return to your earliest memory of who you thought you were or what you thought you were destined to become (this may require a lot of sorting through thoughts and experiences...good and bad). What were the circumstances surrounding you losing your drive? What got you stuck in your comfort zone? Describe the mental chaos it is or was creating for you.

8 BUILDING MENTAL MUSCLE

*W**hen there is no peace, there is no victory*! In other words, dissonance in the three areas of your mindset, create a chaotic vibration that causes you to stay in your own way and it limits your ability to achieve success. So, if there is an internal battle, it will always create an external struggle. And, when things on the outside aren't going right, it points to what is going wrong inside. However, once all three components of your mindset are consistently in alignment, you will have mastered the mental change necessary for reaching your victorious place.

Now, let's be honest. It is not always the enemy that causes the mental chaos. Sometimes, the chaos is the consequence of **our** own actions (notice I included myself because we are **all** subject to this). In the challenge example in chapter one, it was inaction that caused some mental confusion when the pattern was unexpectedly broken. That opened the door for the enemy to send a host of negative thoughts that reinforced the subconscious belief that you would never successfully maintain a consistent work-out regimen. You see, the enemy will capitalize off of the dissonance and continuously throw darts that further perpetuate the mental struggle.

Ephesians 4:27 very clearly instructs us not to "give the devil a foothold." What's a foothold? It is a place in your life or mind that provides stable ground for the enemy to take up residence and make further progress. So, of course, the enemy looks for footholds in your life and in your mindset. He actually "**prowls around** like a roaring lion [fiercely hungry], **seeking** someone to **devour**" (1 Peter 5:8b AMP).

In other words, the devil is <u>restlessly</u> and <u>stealthily</u> HUNTING YOU DOWN! Hopefully, those words are strong enough to get you to truly understand that you are the enemy's prey and he wants you BADLY. If you are not alert at all times, he will sneak up on you, like a thief in the night, and eat you alive. So, take every step towards being well-balanced and disciplined. Make it a priority to get rooted in faith, so you can successfully resist him. Identify when your actions don't line up with your beliefs or God's vision for your life and make a conscious effort to fight for congruence. In addition, get in tune with and redefine your perceptions, thoughts, and feelings, so that they have no control over your behavior. Otherwise you will quickly find yourself in a place of discord unable to hear and obey, regardless of the instructions and promises God has provided.

When discord exists or has been your "normal" for any extended amount of time, you may not even be aware of the mental pandemonium it creates. Many times, it becomes your comfort zone. You have to reach the battle point between your conscious thoughts and subconscious values/beliefs. And, if you are anything like me, you may have to experience a whirlwind of emotions and failed attempts at happiness before you decide to take real action. The problem with that is there are generations of people who desperately need the authentic you to show up, in order to start the process of living out their purpose. It will often take a period of honest and purposeful self-reflection to magnify just how much of a shift your mindset requires. But, rest assured, you can and will reach success and operate in your purpose or vision once you accept that **more is required than chance**. The only path that leads you to your victorious place is conscious CHANGE! You must turn completely away from your old ways and direct your path totally towards God.

Honestly, my friend, the trials and temptations in your life are no different than what others experience, including myself. They may just present themselves to you differently than they present to me or the next person. However, God is faithful. He will never allow you to be tempted beyond your ability. In fact, he promises to show you the way out of every temptation, so that you can endure. I believe that this book is one of the many ways that God is equipping you to build mental muscle and resist the enemy's attacks. So, if you haven't been taking your reading seriously or you have been just skimming over your applicable action points, now is the time to go back. I am encouraging you to start over with an elevated level of expectation.

As previously mentioned, your level of investment in the change process requires a sacrifice and a determination to reevaluate your current situation. I promise when you take an honest look at yourself, then and only then can you do what you need to do to renew your mind. Thoughts rooted in your past and the self-talk that rents space in your mind have very little life-producing influence on the vision that is outlined by your *why (*especially when you have clarity about who you are and what you are here to do in the earth). Furthermore, when you acknowledge that your actions are moving you away from your vision more than towards it, then you are ready to tackle a mindset shift. It takes consistent, ongoing renewal of your conscious mind with the Word and thoughts of God, so don't despise the process. We all fall off the "vision bandwagon", at some point or another, when our peace is attacked. The key is in how we rise up!

Here is the good news. Despite the enemy's tactics to interrupt your peace, you also have a God who created you with the tools and the authority to defeat the enemy's colorful ploys and sneaky deceptions EVERYTIME! In fact, according to the manual in 2 Corinthians 10:3-4 (NLT), "We are human, but we don't wage war as humans do." We actually get to "use God's mighty weapons, not worldly weapons, to knock down the strongholds of human reasoning and to destroy false arguments." There is a biblical truth that tells us that "...we do not wrestle against flesh and blood, but against principalities, against powers, against the rulers of the darkness of this world, against spiritual wickedness in high places" (Ephesians 6:12 KJV). So, this means that nothing that has happened in your life is by coincidence. There is a battle in the unseen realm that directly affects your outcome. It will destroy you, if you don't know who you are.

Simply put, your fight is not against the mom who neglected you or the wife who cheated on you. It is not with the child who won't listen or the father who never acknowledged you. It is also not with the friend who walked away or the one who chose not to fight. They were simply the ones the enemy, the father of lies (John 8:44) skillfully used to cause your doubt, your lack of trust, your anger, your hurt, your trauma and, ultimately, your FEAR. So, change your perception. Truly, the enemy is terrified of the territory that God has assigned to you in the earth. He is aware that, if you finally stumble into the knowledge of who you really are in Christ and release the power of God that is within you, your influence will change the trajectory of multitudes of people and situations. That is why he resorts to these cowardly attempts to deceive you and create chaos in your mind.

However, you do not need to worry or be afraid, especially when you know **whose** you are. In fact, God makes it clear over three hundred times in His word that you do not have to fear. When you have accepted His

Lordship over your life, you can simply bring your concerns to Him in prayer and believe that He will give you every tool necessary to press forward in victory. So, no matter what the enemy attempts to use to stall your progress or paralyze your purpose, rest assured that the battle is already won. God is with you (Deuteronomy 31:6) and He is for you (Romans 8:31), my friend. So, restore your confidence by replacing your fear with the truth of God. It ensures that the enemy has already been rendered powerless (Hebrews 2:14, Colossians 2:15 AMP) and that you are ALREADY victorious (Deuteronomy 20:4).

Your AUTHENTIC SELF and the GOD-GIVEN TRUTH is at the very foundation of your subconscious mind. It is simply hiding under the learned behaviors and habits that your life experiences created. Therefore, taking time to be more mindful of your conscious thinking is truly the most effective way to reprogram your subconscious mind and change your thoughts, beliefs, and behaviors. When you keep God's word at the forefront your mind, this becomes possible.

As is the case with every other muscle in your body, your mind requires constant attention to maintain its strength and operate at full capacity. With the grace of God that empowers you to prosper in every situation and the authority He has given you in the earth, all you have to remember is to stay aligned with His spirit to build your mental muscle. Similar to the time you spend in the gym building physical muscle and shedding off dead weight, constant time with God and application of His word will help you take control of your mind and achieve your vision. The question is, are you willing to put in the work required? I encourage you to take a look at and complete the exercise located in Appendix A, towards the back of the book. It will assist you in laying out a plan to build your mental muscle. Furthermore, it will allow you to operate in the power that God placed deep down in your core, way before you could even think or speak.

"For God has not given us a spirit of fear, but of power and of love and of a sound mind"- 2 Timothy 1:7 (NKJV)

Applicable Action Point

1.) How does your subconscious tend to direct your thoughts and actions most of the time?

2.) Based off the Godly truths that have been shared in this book so far, and the prompting of His spirit that I KNOW is occurring as you are reading through the chapters, what lies have clouded your authentic self and God's truth in your mind?

3.) What unhelpful habits or beliefs are hindering you from pressing into your victorious place? What thoughts are obstructing your ability to identify or carry out God's vision for your life?

4.) What perceptions must you change and what things must you consciously sacrifice to become the man/woman God created you to be?

9 VISUALIZE YOUR WHY

By now you should have a clear understanding that your *why* is essentially your purpose in life. Your vision is what that ***why*** looks like being carried out. And your success in committing to your *why* is rooted in your willingness to outline your day from the moment you open your eyes until the moment you go to bed, with visual representations of your *why*. Visualizing your *why* provides clarity and makes the big picture appear more attainable, causing your perceptions, thoughts, feelings, and behaviors to be in alignment with your overall purpose. When consistently done, the practice of visualization provides the power your mind needs to render those self-defeating thoughts (i.e. fear, worry, procrastination, self-doubt, avoidance, etc.) that attempt to antagonize and taunt your ability to reach your victorious place, **POWERLESS**!

Being clear and tenacious about your *why* also frees you from the bondage of being so focused on your problems that you forget about your reason for working towards success. It truly creates the outward convincing and the inner conviction you need to stay on course. I personally am a huge proponent of creating and utilizing vision boards to visualize your *why* through the intentional use of biblical meditation and your God-given imagination. A vision board is essentially your faith picture. It typically uses quotes and pictures to demonstrate that which you are believing for or whatever is resonating with your spirit and indicates or alludes to the action steps necessary for that belief to come to pass.

When creating a vision board, you can either focus on one or various categories (*i.e.* home, finances, relationships, career, fitness, goal setting, etc.). However, when completing a vision board that focuses on your *why*, I take a bit of a different approach. I host quite a few vision board events per year through my coaching practice, which I entitle "Party with a Purpose". During these events, I encourage participants to dig deeper than cutting out and pasting pictures of fancy cars, ideal bodies, and feel good quotes.

While there is nothing wrong with pasting visuals of fancy cars and firm, fit bodies on your board; the question I ask is: what is the motive behind the pictures you choose? Is it ultimately for you to receive the "ooohs" and "ahhhhs"? Or is it for God to get the glory for what He has doing in your life and the talents and gifts that He has given you to bless others? Now, somebody reading this is probably thinking that I am being too deep and that is understandable. But, in my practice, I find out very quickly who is operating in a place of pride, who is stuck in their comfort zone, or who has no revelation about their *why*...just by what they put on their vision board.

Remember the definition I provided of vision, as it relates to purpose. *Vision is what your why looks like being carried out!* So, having a picture(s) of a fit body, when pertaining to your *why,* might be
 a. a reminder of your need to stay strong and healthy in order to live the longest life possible for carrying out your *why,* or
 b. an indication of the calling or gifts God has given you to carry out your *why* (i.e. a personal trainer or fitness coach).

From the perspective of creating the visual representation of your *why,* there needs to be internal reflection and intentionality. Your vision board will ultimately display what you value most, but the goal is to ensure that it incorporates what the Creator designed you for; thus, I engage my clients in an exercise where they first seek God about whether their desires are in alignment with His will. Prior to even cutting out one picture, they intently examine themselves and answer the following questions:

- How does God want to use you in the earth?
  - In other words, what do you believe that God is asking you to do with your gifts, talents and skills?
- What is God's plan for your purpose?
- What is resonating with your spirit about how, when and where He wants you to carry your purpose out?

How to Use the Board

Unfortunately, the average person doesn't ever complete their board and many never even look at it again after its completion, if they do finish it. The reason this occurs is because a lot of people do not understand or buy-in to the power of the imagination and biblical meditation. In addition, they do not accept the authority God gave His children in Romans 4:17 to speak life over their situations, nor do they heed to the clear instruction God gave to make your vision plain, in Habakkuk 2:2. A major part of my practice is teaching folks how to write the vision and make it plain. This is so important because the reality is, your vision should never end with you! It should be so clear that generations after you can continue to carry it out, in whatever way God designs them to do so.

It is not enough to put your vision board together and continue your same daily routine. You must connect what you see, to what you do, and say it all day long. So, spend time with your board. You can incorporate it in your time with God in the mornings and during your prayer and meditation time before you go to bed at night. Whenever you are faced with a decision, a trial or an opportunity, refer to your board. Be mindful of your feelings as you are reflecting on it in a time of deliberation. Take notice of the alignment of your conscious thoughts with the pictures and phrases God inspired you to paste on the board. Separate the board into smaller sections if you have to and surround yourself with your vision in all the places you frequent throughout the day. You can post it on walls in the bathroom, your office space, the kitchen, etc.

Frequently ask yourself if your choices are bringing you closer to what is on your board or taking you further away from it. And visit your board multiple times throughout the year, as a tool for measuring your goal achievement. Finally, follow your actions with what you speak out of your mouth. Even though you may not be currently living your vision, you will start to attract what you desire with the power of your words. So, remember to constantly "call those things that be not as though they were" (Romans 4:17).

Vision Principles That Drive You into Your Destiny
Experts estimate that the mind thinks somewhere between 60,000-80,0000 thoughts per day. That is an average 2500-3300 thoughts per hour. So, with your brain in constant "go mode" you will obviously need ongoing reminders of the vision that you are working towards, in order to keep it at the forefront of your imagination throughout the day. Once you identify your *why*, this process becomes easier because every action you take moving forward will be motivated by your vision. In other words, once you know where you are going, you can more easily identify what roads will take you there.

With that being said, "vision" can also be likened to "destiny". Your decisions in life determine your destiny; the roadmap you will need to simplify the journey is made plain on your vision board. When your decisions are taking you off course, you will know right away in your daily review of the images on your board because the images outline what you should be working on. Let's take a look at a scenario to help you gain a better understanding:

> *Your vision is to use your gift of creativity in the cosmetology industry. You have already developed your business plan. The only thing holding you back is these last few months of cosmetology school and your licensing exam. However, you are in a season of financial lack. Unhelpful thoughts begin to creep in, repeating such statements as: "you are stupid for not taking that job offer at the bank", "you are in debt" "you will never be successful as an entrepreneur because you can't even handle your bills at home." You begin to remember your financial struggles as a child due to your father's many failed attempts at entrepreneurship. Then you think about your three children and how much you want them to have what they need and want. This is your deciding moment...*

This example provides a great case for the power of a vision board. When you take your time designing it based specifically on your vision, or the destination of your journey, you realize more quickly (in that deciding moment) that finishing school is a road that directly leads there. Taking a job at the bank, unless it can smoothly fit into your plan without you having to quit school, is out of alignment with your vision and counterproductive to your journey.

In this season of intentional living, there is no time for experimentation. You must be goal-directed in your actions and decisions. Your success, my friend, will be determined by your willingness to sacrifice for the vision that you are working towards and your willingness to get uncomfortable on purpose...no matter how painful it is in the process. Your vision board is just another tool to keep your attention on your intention, as you are building that mental muscle to complete the mission.

In your repetitious meditation on the God-inspired words and pictures on your vision board and the completion of each focal area of your vision, you will create new experiences that change your ability to subconsciously believe. The more and more in alignment with your original design and ultimate purpose you become, the more those uninvited mental visitors will lose power over your conscious thinking. Eventually, the renewal of your conscious mind will reprogram the auto pilot of your subconscious mind and direct you into total expectation of what you are believing for. My friend, you will be blown away at how easily you will begin to attract the vision in this process. All things are possible for him who believes and when you imagine what you can do, according to God's will for your life, nothing will be restrained from you (Mark 9:23, Matthew 21:21-22).

"Focus Your Attention on Your Intention!"
-Shannon White, Mindset Coach

CONFRONT YOUR COMFORT, EXCEL IN YOUR PRESS

Shannon T. White, MSW, LCSW, Mindset Coach

MY "WHY" VISION BOARD

Use the space on this and the next page, to write, doodle or paste quotes, scriptures and/or pictures that line up with or represent your WHY...things that will keep your WHY at the forefront of your imagination.

CONFRONT YOUR COMFORT, EXCEL IN YOUR PRESS

NOTE: You can photocopy or print this out (if you have digitally downloaded this book) and keep it somewhere visible all day. This will allow you to reflect on your WHY from the time you wake up until the time you go to bed every day.

10 EQUIPPED FOR THE PRESS

Let me reiterate that you "wrestle not against flesh and blood, but against principalities, against powers, against the rulers of the darkness of the world, against spiritual wickedness in high places" (Ephesians 6:12). Your issues are never as simple as the things you can physically see. Instead, the things going on around you are often just distractions that cause you to lose sight of the real enemy that we discussed in previous chapters. Priscilla Shirer said it best in her book *The Armor of God,* and I quote, "Everything that occurs in the visible, physical world is directly connected to the wrestling match being waged in the invisible, spiritual world."

Priscilla Shirer goes on to suggest that your primary goal is to identify the spiritual truth behind the physical facts and ultimately pin down and defeat him, who is seeking to devour you (1 Peter 5:8). You will lose strength, become vulnerable and lose your competitive advantage if you focus primarily on what you can see in the physical realm *(i.e.* your unruly child or nagging spouse, the person who is trying to stop you, the job you lost, the illness you are fighting, the debt, the break up, your lack of consistency, your control issues or perpetual procrastination, etc.), as opposed to keeping your eyes fixed on the opponent that is warring against you. It is similar to being in the middle of a fist fight and taking your attention off your opponent while you focus on the pain of his last right hook. You will literally get pummeled if you become distracted by the ensuing black eye, instead of fighting back with everything you have within you. You simply must change your perspective and remember that it is not what you see, but the enemy you can't see, that is disrupting your peace.

In your current fight to reaching your victorious place, it is your opponent, the devil, who has tried to keep you in the mental prison of your comfort zone with his lies and cowardly attacks, pretty much all your existence. So, this will be one of the most challenging fights of your life and the victory will not come without a battle that goes beyond your sense of normalcy. But, my friend, you are built for the challenge and EQUIPPED FOR THE PRESS! Your task in this battle will be to filter years of conscious thoughts and feelings through the word of God, change your perceptions to create new experiences, and develop a plan for the immediate elimination and replacement of every subconscious thought that is holding you captive (2 Corinthians 10:4-5). It will not be a quick fix or a "one and done" effort, nor will you be able to simply "enter the ring" once a week or only when you face difficult situations. It will be a continuous bout.

It is *in* God's truth about how He made you and His power that He placed inside of you, that will help you achieve the win and replace every lie that has taken residence in you. It is in your intimate time with Him, that God will reveal to you every mystery and answer that you require to succeed. Remember, He literally created you in His likeness and image. He put TRUTH in you before you were even conceived, so He can certainly bring it back to your revelation if you just sit and commune with Him.

When you work tenaciously to get back to your original design, you magnetize that core truth that has been overshadowed by lies all these years. God's word becomes your new inner voice, or your new subconscious autopilot. There is truly a spirit of liberation that occurs when you are willing to exchange your fleshy perspective for God's spiritual perspective. You will no longer walk around in fear or with a need for control, nor will you find the need to strive for perfection or approval from others. The old rhetoric and lies of your past will no longer have power over your thinking or your sense of self. You get to a place of legitimately being gratified with where you are in life, and in who you are because you now have understanding that it will be used to glorify God through your purpose.

In addition, when the seasons of your life change, as they will, you will naturally accept the evolution that comes with movement from one stage to the next. I will warn you that there will be some difficult days and sometimes painful self- reflection and letting go. It will require forgiveness of yourself and others, but it will be perfectly possible **when and if you make a conscious decision** to spend intimate time learning who you are in the eyes of

God and who you are called to be according to His purpose for your life. Yes, when you sacrifice your time and surrender yourself to God through <u>consistent praying</u> (1 Thessalonians 5:17 NASB), <u>meditating</u> on the word and <u>quieting your mind</u> (Psalm 4:4 NASB) to <u>listen</u> to the still voice of His spirit (Matthew 11:15 MSG):

- **emotions** that you once believed had power over you **become powerless**,
- **strongholds** on your life weaken and eventually **break**,
- **thoughts/actions** that are out of alignment with your *why* begin to **change direction and line up** with that which is required by your original design,
- **motivation increases**, and
- the **desire to walk in your destiny becomes stronger** than the false comfort of familiarity.

Once you accept how impactful you are in your authentic, purpose-filled self, no uninvited mental visitor or past influence will stop you from actively pressing towards your goals. Why? Because your subconscious mind, once reprogrammed to its original state (fashioned after God), will now have the authority to convince your conscious thoughts that you are powerful beyond measure. In turn, your actions will line up accordingly.

Every self-sabotaging thought of fear and doubt, worry and sadness, will come under the subjection of your inner voice and be replaced by the truth of how God authentically sees and created you:

You are shaped and formed in the likeness and image of God. Thus, every thought must obey <u>He</u> who lives in you (Genesis 1:26-27; 2 Corinthians 10:5). Your conscious thoughts must acknowledge and "fall in line", when your underlying subconscious truth steps on the scene. Fleshy thoughts simply have no power over the authentic truth of your God-inspired core beliefs (unless you give them the power).

You are fearfully and wonderfully made (Psalm 139:14), *God's handiwork* (Ephesians 2:10), and there is nothing wrong with you. You are **exactly** who you are supposed to be! Your past, your perceived weaknesses, and your flaws will all be used by God to develop your story. He did not allow you to go through anything that He didn't think you were capable of handling or that wouldn't benefit your testimony. In fact, He used it to qualify you for the position.

You are the head and not the tail...above and not beneath (Deuteronomy 28:13), so there is no situation powerful enough to take you off course. When you keep God's truth (which is at the core of your subconscious) at the forefront of your imagination (your conscious mind), every enemy is defeated, and you always rise to the top.

You can do ALL things through Him (Phil 4:13), so always remember that your sky has no limit. There is no cap to your potential and your vision has the capacity to stretch well beyond human conceptualization.

You are complete in Him (Colossians 2:10) and everything you need to accomplish your vision is already wrapped up on the inside of you. He prepared your specific vision *in advance for you to fulfill and gave you the capacity walk it out* (Ephesians 2:10).

God's original plan was for man (including you and me) to **dominate** here on the earth, **give life** to what He had created for us and **exceed our perceived capacity** by fully functioning in the power that He put in us when He formed and intricately wove us together. How do I know that? Well take a look at Genesis 1:27-28 which tells us that God created man [male and female] **in His own image**…and said unto them, Be fruitful, and multiply, and replenish the earth, and **subdue it and have dominion**…" Then Genesis 2:19 says, "…out of the ground the Lord God formed every beast of the field, and every fowl of the air; and **brought them unto Adam to see what he would call them**: and **whatsoever** Adam called every living creature, **that was the name** thereof".

The key to understanding all of this and ultimately gaining clarity about your innate power is Genesis 2:7, where it says that God "…breathed into [Adam's] nostrils the **breath of life**; and man became a **living soul**." (Note: the Hebrew word for "soul" in this passage is *nephesh*). So, when God "created man in His own image" and breathed life into him, the Creator essentially breathed **Himself** into the body of the man that He made. Therefore, Adam **became** *nephesh*. He became a living, speaking spirit, like

God, possessing a mind, emotions, will, intellect, personality and a conscience.

When God later created the animals, He brought them to Adam, allowing Adam to fully operate in his creativity and authority by naming each of them. Every beast became **just** what Adam spoke over its life or what he called them.

Now take a second to really think about that. When you consider all the animals and living creatures on the earth, don't you think Adam had to have a pretty extensive vocabulary to name every single one of them? Not only did God anoint Adam with the capacity to complete such a great assignment, but He granted him the authority to literally identify the characteristics of each animal. If Adam was the original design for man, that must mean that you too have a brain capacity that is limitless in its natural state. But, your environment, the people around you, the repetitive information you hear, and your experiences has skewed or diminished it.

However, now that you are aware that there is no limit on your life, that your authentic design is to dominate in the earth and that you have the capacity to create and name your situations, the influences that shaped your belief system can be laid to rest. Allow the truth, that says "you are complete in God", to set you free and provide the confidence you need to think bigger. In time, your actions will follow suit. You can no longer rely on the excuse that you don't have an example, because Jesus is your example. Furthermore, EVERYTHING you need to know about ANYTHING you might face in life has already been written and accounted for in the manual.

In retrospect, your beliefs pinpoint your misalignment. So, pay attention to the areas where you are too comfortable and where you are not in line with what God says about who you are and what you are capable of accomplishing. It could truly be what causes you to detour or even teeter and tumble off that wagon we discussed before. All you have to do then is re-program your thinking and return to your original design if you want to excel in your press.

When you:

1. **ReNew, ReIGNITE, and ReCommit** to God's vision for your life,

2. **Meditate on it daily**, consistently making the truth your confession, and

3. **Press forward in faith** ensuring that every action corresponds with your vision...*YOU WIN*!!!

Thus, *whatever season of your overall why that you are in,* will become more defined and victory driven. Instead of focusing on your resolutions, it now becomes about living to carry out your innate purpose.

Now, do me a big favor and take a look at Appendix B before you complete the final Applicable Action Point. I simply want you to take a moment to reflect on who you are. In the spirit of keeping God's truth at the forefront of your imagination, I want you start with some declarations and scriptural references that provide you with evidence that you are **EQUIPPED FOR THE PRESS**. After you have finished the applicable action point, I would like you to go back to Appendix B and write your own declaration and specific scriptures you would like to remember, based on the revelation you have received from reading this book and completing the written exercises. This will help your journey to become more personalized and internally driven.

Until we meet again, please know that I believe in your ability to carry out God's vision for your life. Your victorious place is right around the corner. It is what you become by finishing, that makes the sacrifice worth it. Remember – Confront Your Comfort, Excel in Your Press! There is Victory in Your Vision!

> *"...As for you, if you live in my presence...pure in heart and action, living the life I've set out for you, attentively obedient to my guidance and judgments, then I'll back your kingly rule...make it a sure thing on a sure foundation."*
> - 2 Chronicles 7:17-18 MSG

CONFRONT YOUR COMFORT, EXCEL IN YOUR PRESS

Applicable Action Point- Note to Self: Who Am I?

AFTERWORD

You have been armored with some amazing, life changing strategies for confronting your comfort in this book and hopefully you are more confident in your ability to excel in your press. However, there is one more vital key to unlocking the door to your victorious place. In writing this book, I am on assignment from God. Therefore, I could not end until I made sure that you were at least exposed to or given access to the key that I am referring to. Unfortunately, you cannot fully operate in your God-given authority or God's vision for your life, if you do not have a living relationship with Jesus Christ. So, if you have never officially declared Jesus Christ as the Lord and Savior of your life, here is your chance.

The book of Genesis discusses the consequences of the fall of the original man, Adam. Unfortunately for mankind, Adam's disobedience locked the door to the kingdom, prohibiting us from walking in the authority that God intended for his children. Adam was given the master key by God, but he handed it over to the enemy when he fell for the devil's lies.

However, there is good news! You, my friend, are the apple of God's eye and because of how much God loves you, He sent his only begotten son Jesus, to destroy the works of the devil on your behalf (1 John 3:8) and to reveal God's true love and forgiving nature to you. Jesus literally walked out his *why* in the earth, just as you and I are required to do, providing a perfect example of God's vision fulfilled.

In John 10:10, Jesus said, *"I came that they may have life and have it abundantly"* - a complete life full of purpose. When Jesus died on the cross, an exchange took place in which Jesus took on mankind's sin and gave mankind His righteousness (the gift of "right standing" with God). Jesus' obedience to God's call on His life, allowed Him to snatch the master key back from the devil, so He could return a copy to each of God's children (the rightful owners). It is a free gift that unlocks your original design and the power that goes with it. Unfortunately, contrary to popular belief, you will never be able to earn this access by your works alone. So just "being a good person" does not entitle you to the key. You must genuinely accept the Gift-giver and His free gift of righteousness.

I invite you to take a step of faith and pray the following prayer. The only <u>requirements</u> are that it come from your heart and that you confess it with your mouth. Romans 10:9-10 (NIV) says that "if you declare with your mouth, 'Jesus is Lord,' and believe in your heart that God raised him from the dead, you will be saved. For it is with your heart that you believe and are justified, and it is with your mouth that you profess your faith and are saved."

> **Dear God,**
>
> *I confess that I am a sinner. For much too long, I have tried to do things my way and have ignored your desire to be ruler over my life. I no longer want anything else to take your place, so today I repent of my sins and ask that you forgive me. I believe that you sent your son, Jesus, and that He died on the cross in exchange for my sins. I also believe that you raised Him from the dead and He now sits, very much alive, at the right hand of your throne interceding on my behalf. I completely accept Him as my personal Lord and Savior and receive your free gift of salvation and righteousness. From this day forward, I give you full access to guide my life and lead me in doing your will. Thank you for allowing Jesus to come into my life, give me the key to the kingdom, and position me as joint heir to the throne. Thank you for setting me free.*
>
> *In Jesus' name I pray,*
Amen

_____   _____
Signature   Date

If you have prayed this prayer in sincere faith, you may want to sign your name under the prayer and include today's date as a reminder of your new birth. You have come to Christ in faith, trusting him as your Lord and Savior. You are now a new creation, in right standing with God and no longer guilty of your sin-filled past. When you mess up (and you will, because we all do), just get back up, repent and continue to walk towards God.

You literally have all the help you need to succeed, because God's Holy Spirit (Acts 16-18), the same power that raised Christ from the dead, now resides on the inside of you. It will give you the strength to rise up, out of every dead situation you face. Heaven is now your eternal home, so death no longer has any power over your current life. With that being said, there is nothing that you set your mind to do, if it is in alignment with the word of God, that is impossible. Congratulations my friend. Welcome to the family!

Here are four crucial things you will need to stay on track, as you watch the blessing of your decision unfold before your eyes:

Pray: Start talking to God TODAY! Remember that you are now in relationship with Him and constant communication is vital for growth in any relationship.

> *"It's not the prayer that saves; it's the repentance and faith behind the prayer that lays hold of salvation"*
> - J.D Greerer

Bible: Start reading your bible to build your faith and renew your mind with the word of God. Faith comes by hearing and hearing the word of God.

Church Home: Get connected to a good bible believing, bible teaching church that will show you how to grow in the word.

Community Accountability: Begin to forge relationships with other people that are living for God. "As iron sharpens, so one man sharpens [and influences] another [through discussion]." Proverbs 27:17 (AMP).

"And the life I now live in the flesh I live by faith in the Son of God, who loved me and gave himself for me."
Galatians 2:20b ESV

APPENDIX A: Mental Muscle Workout Plan

Note: This is a suggested format; however, I encourage you to do what works best for you. Also, keep a separate daily journal or log to help keep you focused over the time period it will take you to build your mental muscle. It will keep you honest, help you to find patterns in your thinking, push you harder, assist you in maintaining a visual of your goals, build your spiritual confidence and give you a place to vent your frustrations with the process. I suggest that you repeat this routine daily for at least 45-60 days until it becomes an unconscious habit. Remember change is a process that comes with repetition. There may be setbacks and some days will seem more difficult than others. The key is for you to do the work and trust God for the continued revelation.

1. **Pre-Workout Routine**:
    a. Identify a time that you can consistently devote to your workout, between 15-20 minutes per day—remember the "I" (investment) of I.R.A. Your outcome will be determined by the level of your investment or sacrifice.
    b. Prepare your "equipment", or lay out what you will need the night before (ensure that your quiet space is clear of clutter, that your bible, reading material, journal, pen, music

playlist, highlighter, etc. is in one accessible location in your quiet space

c. Enter your "gym" (your identified quiet location, prayer closet, etc.) with a spirit of expectation and a resolve to reset your thinking. This space should be free of distractions (which means you might want to leave any access to emails, texts, and social media in another room).

d. Set the atmosphere. I usually ask God to clear the atmosphere and let Him know that He is welcome into the room (this place can also be a patio, a park bench, or wherever you consistently go when you need peace), as I play my Christian Worship music to help me get focused.

e. Sit quietly and read your journal entry from the day prior. This serves as a reminder of the goals you have set and the progress you have made in adjusting your thinking so far.

2. **Warm-up**:
   a. Thank God for His time, sacrifice, mercy and grace, which allows you full access to him and empowers you to prosper through the process of growth.
   b. Ask for His wisdom and discernment concerning who He created you to be and the areas of your thinking that are out of line with the vision.

c. Declare your freedom from the lies of the enemy and your acceptance of the promises that God has already given you to negate those lies.
d. Date your journal for the current day revelation.

3. **Stretching**: After reviewing previous revelation and thinking about your application of that revelation the day before, begin to identify areas that need continued work and more training. Make note of those areas, picking out key words/struggles that have been at the forefront of your mind. You may very well work on the same thought for a week straight or the whole 45-60 days and that is okay because it probably took a lifetime for it to become a part of your subconscious thinking patterns. God will give you different techniques for building the muscle in that area.

4. **Active weight training**: In this process you will feel like some of what you have to face weighs entirely more than you can bear. But remember, just as when you are working out to build physical muscle, your mind is a lot more capable of increasing in its strength than you think. It is truly mind over matter…God's truth over the perceived "facts". Subconsciously, you can always press a little more than you think you can. I suggest that you only focus on one to two thoughts for this next

45-60 days that need to be renewed. This will allow you to focus on those thoughts, little by little, every day in your daily workout.

As you focus on renewing your mind, use your daily journal entry to write a reflection of where you are mentally and spiritually with the thought(s) you are working on. Elaborate on your perceptions, feelings and actions regarding the thought(s). In addition, it is good practice to write down what you hear God saying in your intimate time with Him (particularly in regard to His instructions for combatting those mental infiltrators we discussed in Chapter seven).

5. **Post-Workout Stretch**: This part of the work-out will last the remainder of your day. In order to avoid the extra stress on your body following any workout, you must stretch afterwards. So, for purposes of building your mental muscle, you will stretch the knowledge you received in your active weight training by continuing to pray throughout the day and by meditating on the scriptures and the positive affirmations God gave you in his time with him.

6. **Meal Prep**: Finally, in order to increase your ability to maintain your new habit outside of your time with God, it is important to always have your mental muscle diet prepared and ready. It will limit your urge to feast on the music, reading material,

conversations, *etc.* that reinforce old thoughts, beliefs and behaviors. Remember you are in training mode right now and until you are more mentally fit, there are certain carnal things you will need to replace or avoid while you are building your muscle.

Every morning when I wake up, I have my phone set to send me a notification with the Scripture of the Day from my bible app. Sometimes, that is just the scripture that I need to motivate me for my daily mental muscle workout. When I am trying to remember a specific behavior or encouraging thought, I type it into the notes feature of my phone. I have also used notecards and post-it notes to keep the Word readily available when I am feeling spiritually, mentally or emotionally light-headed throughout the day.

You can always rely on a positive message on a sticky note placed on your desk at work or on the inside of your wallet or day planner. It is truly the perfect appetizer while waiting for your lunch break. Plan ahead for your car rides or running errands by replacing your normal playlist with motivational speakers, inspirational podcasts, faith-filled sermons, e-books, or some encouraging/ relaxing music. A small devotional book, that you can carry in your purse or pocket, is always a great healthy snack to pull out during your train ride home or in the waiting room at your doctor's appointment. Having truth declarations posted in various places in your home, particularly the bathroom mirror, provides a wonderful night cap. The point is to have enough truth, visibly available at all times of the day, to eradicate the lies causing your mental chaos. A steady, well-balanced diet of the Word of God will accomplish just that.

Remember, muscle development occurs when exercise is consistent, challenging and long-term. Muscles truly respond to good form and repetition. And as you continually challenge your muscles to deal with higher levels of resistance or weight, they steadily grow.

Similarly, if you commit the next 45-60 days to follow this plan, you will build your mental muscle. Consistently challenging your thoughts will essentially develop a new and healthy mindset. This may appear to be a heavy, burdensome task. However, I can assure you that it will be the most valuable in building the muscle needed to eliminate mental chaos as you press towards your victorious place. Furthermore, it is the absolute most effective way of showing the enemy that he no longer controls your peace, nor does he have free access to your mind.

APPENDIX B: Declarations and Scriptural References

My Victory Declaration

Because I walk with God, talk with God and am consumed with God, I am His treasure. I am filled with His love and empowered by His grace. His oil saturates every dry area of my life and His partnership gives me the weapons I need to overcome every trick of the enemy.

I am victorious over my thoughts. So, whatever I can conceive & believe, I can achieve. In fact, ALL things are possible to me because I BELIEVE! My capabilities and potential are unlimited. I push past my comfort zone and stretch the capacity of my vision more and more each day.

I see problems as preparation for my purpose. As I vigorously climb the mountain to my destiny, I see challenges as steppingstones that lead me to grow stronger in faith and focus.

I have creative authority in the earth. Everything I touch prospers and my thoughts are illuminated by the light and wisdom of God. I vividly visualize myself as the person I was created to be. I release and let go of the things outside of my authentic self, and enthusiastically take the action steps necessary to press forward into VICTORY!

My Difference Maker Declaration

According to Jude 20-23, I will build myself up in most holy faith and stay in the center of God's love. I will keep my arms open and outstretched, ready for God's instructions for my direction in life and accepting of His mercy for my shortcomings.

I will constantly and consistently perform the work expected of me by God, with due diligence. I will go easy on those who hesitate in faith and go after and snatch up those who take the wrong way. I will exhibit the spirit of gentleness with sinners, but I will attack their sin viciously in the Spirit.

I trust God to keep me on my feet. I trust Him to multiply my power with His own. I trust that I am surrounded and protected for every moment of this journey by His heavenly hosts.

Because I seek the kingdom of God and all of its righteousness FIRST, I am fully confident that God approves of my life, causing even my enemies to end up shaking my hand (Proverbs 16:7). I am today and for the rest of my life, a kingdom difference maker. When I walk into a room or step into a situation, I make a difference because of my connection to God and because of the leading of the Holy Spirit through me. I AM THE ANSWER!

According to Proverbs 16:7, God's Spirit is on me. He has chosen me to preach the message of good news to the poor, sent me to announce pardon to the prisoners, and recovery of sight to the blind, to set the burdened and battered free, to announce "this is God's year to act!" Therefore, I declare that scripture WILL make history in my life this year!

Scriptural References

Psalm 119:59 (NSV) "I pondered the direction of my life, and I turned to follow your laws"

Lamentations 3:40 (NASB) "Let us examine and probe our ways and let us return to the Lord"

Psalm 119:105 (KJV) "Thy word is a lamp unto my feet, and a light unto my path"

Proverbs 23:7 (KJV) "As a man thinketh in his heart, so is he"

1 Thessalonians 5:17 (NASB) "Pray without ceasing"

Psalm 4:4 (NASB) "…Meditate in your heart upon your bed and be still. Selah"

Matthew 11:15 (MSG) "Are you listening to me? Really listening?"

Psalm 35:1, 23 (NIV) "Contend Lord with those who contend with me; fight against those who fight against me… Awake and rise to my defense! Contend for me, my God and Lord."

John 3:16 (KJV) "God so loved the world that He gave His one and only Son [Jesus Christ], that whoever believes in Him shall not perish, but have eternal life"

John 10:10 Jesus said, "I came that they may have life and have it abundantly"- a complete life full of purpose".

My Personal Declaration

My Favorite Scriptures

POINTS TO REMEMBER FOR INDIVIDUAL REFLECTION OR GROUP DISCUSSION

CONFRONT YOUR COMFORT, EXCEL IN YOUR PRESS

Made in the USA
Columbia, SC
10 November 2022